A MAN WITH CRIMINALITY SENSATIONS

THE BIOGRAPHY OF AEMIOZLYN D. RUSIO

GAURAV PALIWAL

Copyright © Gaurav Paliwal
All Rights Reserved.

This book has been self-published with all reasonable efforts taken to make the material error-free by the author. No part of this book shall be used, reproduced in any manner whatsoever without written permission from the author, except in the case of brief quotations embodied in critical articles and reviews.

The Author of this book is solely responsible and liable for its content including but not limited to the views, representations, descriptions, statements, information, opinions and references ["Content"]. The Content of this book shall not constitute or be construed or deemed to reflect the opinion or expression of the Publisher or Editor. Neither the Publisher nor Editor endorse or approve the Content of this book or guarantee the reliability, accuracy or completeness of the Content published herein and do not make any representations or warranties of any kind, express or implied, including but not limited to the implied warranties of merchantability, fitness for a particular purpose. The Publisher and Editor shall not be liable whatsoever for any errors, omissions, whether such errors or omissions result from negligence, accident, or any other cause or claims for loss or damages of any kind, including without limitation, indirect or consequential loss or damage arising out of use, inability to use, or about the reliability, accuracy or sufficiency of the information contained in this book.

Made with ♥ on the Notion Press Platform
www.notionpress.com

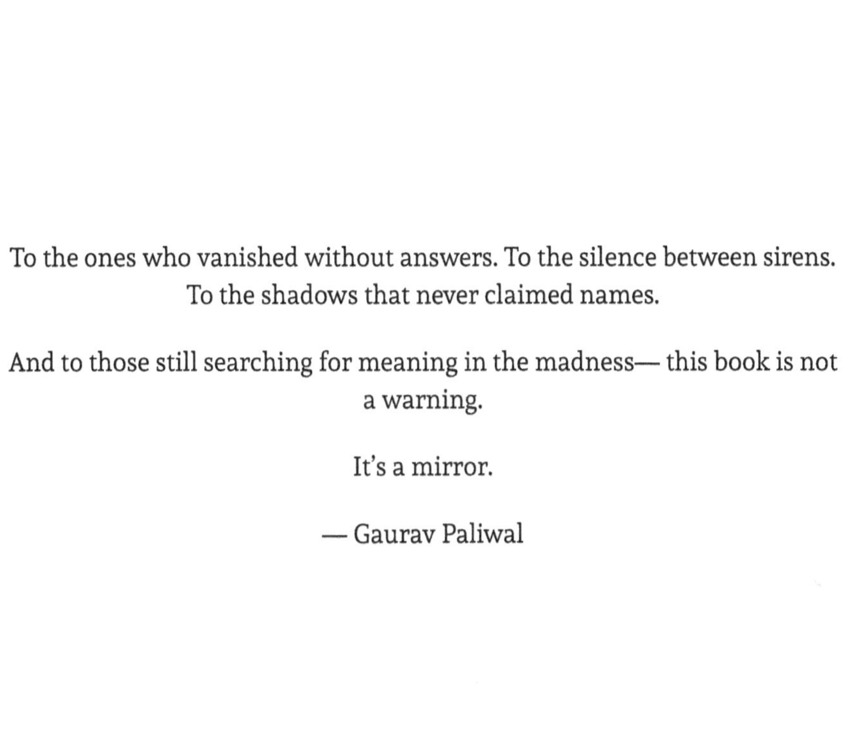

To the ones who vanished without answers. To the silence between sirens.
To the shadows that never claimed names.

And to those still searching for meaning in the madness— this book is not
a warning.

It's a mirror.

— Gaurav Paliwal

Contents

Contents

Foreword

There are books that challenge, books that inspire, and then there are books that haunt. A Man With Criminality Sensations belongs in the latter category—except this book doesn't haunt you when you read it. It haunts you afterward. It lives in your hallway mirror, in your midnight footsteps, in the way your phone flickers when no one's calling. This isn't a tale. It's a trap.

In writing this foreword, I was warned by more than one person. Advised to step away. To not even open the pages of the manuscript that had already left a trail of paranoia among early editors, designers, and researchers. One of them—the last I spoke to—said, "This book breathes wrong. It knows you." He hasn't been heard from since.

So why, then, did I continue? Why write this foreword at all? The answer is simple and terrifying: we cannot afford not to understand him. Aemiozlyn D. Rusio is not merely a criminal. He is not a mind to be diagnosed, dissected, or dismissed. He is a mirror of everything the human mind tries to suppress: chaos, cruelty, and consequence wrapped in one soul-sized anomaly.

This biography is unlike any you've read. Not only because of the content—which veers from forensic horror to metaphysical dread—but because of the way it resists comprehension. Chapters collapse logic. Names vanish after you highlight them. And the more you read, the more your own memories begin to shimmer with uncertainty. Did you always lock that door at night? Was the hallway light always so dim?

Aemiozlyn D. Rusio's life—or what can be reconstructed of it—is a sequence of unanswered questions masquerading as crimes. He killed over 450 people, yet never in the same way. Some died without wounds. Others lived without bodies. One victim's heart was found beating inside a grandfather clock—still ticking, long after death. Another man was buried standing up, eyes wide open, facing the sunrise, with a smile carved into his chest. And still, not one motive. Not one clue as to why.

But that's the mystery. That's what this book seeks to illuminate—not with answers, but with shadows shaped like truth. Each chapter peels back the skin of normalcy and exposes the circuitry of horror beneath. You will not find clarity here. What you will find is a thread—subtle, elusive, and perhaps fatal. A thread that, if pulled long enough, may lead you to where Aemiozlyn walks now.

There is no denying the danger of this book. I've read it. I've written this foreword with a candle lit in a room of mirrors, surrounded by salt lines and silence. Laugh if you must. But when you read on, do so knowing this: the book does not forget. It watches. It follows. It changes you.

And if you feel eyes reading with you—don't look behind you.

— Anonymous Contributor (Some names refuse to stay printed)

They told me not to write this book. Some whispered warnings. Others screamed them. Scholars of criminal psychology, spiritualists, detectives, archivists, even convicts—all begged me to abandon this pursuit. "There are stories that don't want to be told," one said. Another warned, "You write about him long enough, and he'll start writing back." But I couldn't stop. Because this is not just a story. This is the only surviving truth.

A Man With Criminality Sensations is not written in celebration. It is written in defiance of forgetting. It is an act of resistance against the fading, fragmented whispers that Aemiozlyn D. Rusio has left in his wake. The name—unknown to the average citizen—haunts the margins of police reports, the ends of death certificates, the corrupted files in international criminal databases. No image. No birth certificate. No fingerprints. Just a sequence of actions that cannot be ignored.

For years, I collected the un-collectible: rumors, dead-end reports, hidden psychiatric evaluations, censored photographs, survivor notes, coded graffiti, and odd ritualistic documents. Every piece of evidence I found contradicted another. Every fact buried itself beneath layers of absurdity. But when you step far enough back from the noise, patterns begin to emerge. Horrific, undeniable patterns.

I didn't write this book in a conventional way. There were no interviews in bright-lit cafes. No archival institutions offered me guidance. I didn't sit at a desk and calmly draft chapters. I wrote most of it in motion—while relocating, while hiding, while watching things I couldn't unsee. Entire paragraphs were typed on a train that had no stops. Sections were edited by candlelight because no electric light would remain stable when I spoke his name aloud. This biography—if that's even what we can call it—is not a product of research. It is a product of survival.

Why write it, then? Why feed the myth? Why risk my own name, my own safety, my own sleep?

Because there is a terrifying gap in the collective narrative of our time, and his presence fills it. He is not fiction. He is not a legend crafted to scare children. He is what exists when trauma does not find voice, when pain evolves without empathy, when identity is built not on love or memory, but pure rejection. Aemiozlyn D. Rusio is not simply the world's most dangerous criminal. He is the reflection of everything the world fails to acknowledge.

And now, through these pages, he watches you watch him.

This book will not tell you where he is now. It will not give you the relief of resolution. Instead, it will offer you something far worse:

Understanding.

You will understand the way he planned. The way he moved. The sounds he left behind. The strange synchronicities that follow his trail. The way cities bend slightly in his presence. The names of those who got too close. And the reason people who seek his truths often cease to exist, not just physically, but in memory. Entire friend circles forgetting they ever knew someone. Whole offices erasing records of coworkers. Families losing faces from photo frames.

And still, I wrote. Because fear must be documented. Because truth, even poisonous, demands to be seen. Because the next person he chooses may read these very words.

So I leave you with a warning disguised as an invitation: Read carefully. Read in daylight. Do not speak his name aloud. And if you begin to feel the room quiet when it should not... if your technology glitches on one name alone... if your reflection looks slightly off when you finish a chapter...

Put the book down. And remember: this was never meant for entertainment.

It was meant as a record.

And now that you are part of that record... he may already be writing you into the next chapter.

— Gaurav Paliwal

Acknowledgements

Writing A Man With Criminality Sensations was not simply a creative journey—it was a descent. A surrender to shadows. A willingness to wade knee-deep through stories most would refuse to believe, let alone revisit. And in that darkness, there were still echoes of guidance, encouragement, and support that I must pause to acknowledge.

First, I extend profound thanks to the readers—past, present, and future—who dared to open these pages, knowing what kind of name lingered within them. You are not just readers; you are explorers of psychological ruin, witnesses to unspeakable phenomena, and companions in this quiet terror. Without your thirst for truth beyond the surface, this story would remain buried and fragmented.

To the shadows behind the research—anonymous, quiet, persistent. You know who you are. You offered fragments, encrypted files, untraceable phone calls, and whispers in hallways I never entered. Each piece became a bone in the skeleton of this story. You asked for no credit, and in many cases, no contact—but your fingerprints are in every chapter, every scream.

To the historians and investigators who chased the myth of Aemiozlyn D. Rusio before me and vanished into the silence of disbelief: your absence spoke louder than your discoveries. I studied the files you never closed, followed trails you etched in invisible ink. This book is, in some small way, your unfinished statement made whole.

A heartfelt thank you to those who supported me emotionally and creatively during the darkest writing hours. To the fellow writers who dared read drafts and returned with haunted expressions, torn notes, and one warning: "This might be too real." You made this more than fiction—you made it convincing.

To my friends who tolerated my late-night absences, one-word replies, and obsession with symbology, forensic timelines, and whispering patterns—thank you for grounding me in the ordinary when I floated too long in the abyss.

To the artists who helped visualize this world with shadow, distortion, and abstract horror—your work carried the atmosphere of this book in a way my words never could alone. The cover, the icons, the textures of decay—each image bleeds alongside the prose.

To the anonymous sources who claimed to have seen him, spoken to him, escaped him—I cannot verify your truth, but I felt the sincerity of your fear. Whether fabricated, hallucinated, or authentic, your testimonies added haunting realism to the life of someone who is not just hard to find, but impossible to follow.

To my family—thank you for allowing me the space to write something that often made me emotionally distant and mentally scattered. Your support was the anchor in the sea of unreality.

And finally, to Aemiozlyn D. Rusio—if you are indeed reading this, if these pages somehow passed through your hands or your gaze, then perhaps this book serves not as a warning, but as a mirror you once avoided. This is not a tribute. This is not praise. This is documentation—a surgical, violent truth woven in fiction's clothing. You are not forgotten.

You are feared.

This work exists because some stories demand to be told, even if their endings cost us peace. And if the act of knowing your name is dangerous, then so be it. Some horrors deserve the dignity of a witness.

— Gaurav Paliwal

Prologue

It begins not with a scream, but with the absence of one.

Somewhere, sometime—though the exact place remains lost to fog and fractured memory—a family of four simply vanished. They lived in a modest house, the kind with yellow wallpaper that curled at the edges and a rusted wind chime that never sang. One morning, the postman noticed the newspapers piling up. By the third day, a neighbor called the authorities. When they entered the home, they found dinner on the table—plates still warm. Lights flickering. A record spinning on the player, the needle caught in an endless loop of static. No signs of struggle. No forced entry. Just four chairs pulled slightly back from the table, as if their occupants had only stood up to stretch.

And on the mirror in the hallway, etched in something that wasn't quite blood and wasn't quite ink: "You heard him too late."

This was the first of many.

But it wasn't until much later that the name Aemiozlyn D. Rusio would appear in connection with these absences. Before that, he existed only as a ghost in the data, a smear in video surveillance, a whisper in classified reports. The pattern was always the same: he was nowhere and everywhere, present only in his aftermath. Crime scenes left no bodies. Only impressions. Like fingerprints pressed into fog.

This book was not written from police reports or autopsy files. No official agency could ever hold onto the truth long enough to report it. The ones who tried—journalists, whistleblowers, even psychics—either disappeared or turned violently mad. A man in Montreal who traced Rusio's movement across five European countries was found with his own eyes removed and a phrase scrawled across his chest in braille: "Don't look where I've been."

Those brave or foolish enough to keep digging found that Aemiozlyn's crimes were not bound by motive or logic. He killed indiscriminately—doctors, priests, beggars, CEOs. But each death was like a puzzle piece that didn't fit. Unconnected. Until you stopped looking at the individuals and began to trace the shapes between them. The symbols. The repetition of unspeakable things. The patterns of pain.

What you're holding now is the first—and perhaps final—attempt to stitch these impossibilities into a single narrative. It's more than a biography. It's a ritual. Every chapter brings you closer not to an answer, but to an understanding. Not of who Aemiozlyn D. Rusio is, but what he means.

Because you see, there's a reason no place remembers birthing him. No mother claims him. No tombstone waits for him. Aemiozlyn isn't bound by the rules of nature. He doesn't leave tracks. He leaves trauma. He moves through belief and memory like a virus. You don't find him. He finds you.

And he only finds those who know to look.

The accounts in this book were gathered through whispers, forbidden archives, and first-hand testimonies from those who should no longer be breathing. Some of the pages you'll read may change as you read them. Some names will blur. Some sentences will disappear. That is not an error. That is Aemiozlyn.

He is not a man. He is a consequence. A curse that adapts.

So why publish this book at all?

Because sometimes the only way to protect the world from a predator is to name it. To bring it into the light, even if it burns everything around it. Because for too long, he has fed on silence.

And because, maybe—just maybe—you are not like the others.

Maybe you will read this not with fear, but with fire. With purpose. With the kind of obsession that makes you dangerous.

But be warned: once you know him, you are no longer safe.

He has a rule. A single, elegant rule:

"If they know me, they are mine."

Now you know him.

And he knows you.

1

The Child Born in Absence

There are no records. No hospitals. No warm photographs of a mother's arms or a father's name whispered with pride. The first tragedy of Aemiozlyn D. Rusio's existence is that his birth was not a beginning—it was a fracture. A slash in the timeline of the world that began without ceremony, without witnesses, and without origin. To this day, no map bears a mark where he was first held. No land claims the curse of creating him. He was not found—he *appeared*.

Stories about his arrival are scattered, contradictory, sometimes fantastical. An old priest from Hungary claims he once held a silent infant in a bundle of scorched linens left at the base of a crumbling chapel. A woman from Buenos Aires insists she saw a boy of six crawl from a drain one summer night, pale as moonlight, smiling with missing teeth that had never grown in. A retired police chief in Belarus swears the name "Aemiozlyn" came across his desk in a sealed case file from 1974—a year before the supposed child should have even existed.

And yet, all their accounts echo the same truth: **no one remembers the moment he became real. Only the moments he began to erase others.**

His childhood—what little can be pieced together—is defined by anomalies. There were no school records. No vaccinations. No neighbors who recall a playful boy. He did not cry in the night or leave toys behind. But entire **buildings emptied** when he passed through. Whole **towns forgot** names of children they had raised beside him. And always, always, he was gone before he was caught.

At the age of nine—if age even applies—his first confirmed appearance emerged in the surveillance footage of a warehouse fire in Belgium. Flames reflected in his eyes, but he held no matches. The fire chief died two nights later, tongue removed and replaced with a folded blueprint of the facility. In the corner of that blueprint: a name scrawled in red chalk—**Rusio.**

But this was only the whisper. The breath before the scream.

Aemiozlyn's adolescence was marked by **disappearances**, not crimes. Entire subway cars full of people never arriving at their next station. A department store in Sweden shuttered forever after thirty-two shoppers were found sitting in silence, unmoving, eyes filled with dust, **as if they had aged in a moment.** No fingerprints. No motive. Only a phrase etched into a dressing room mirror: *"Watch me disappear."*

As he grew—or evolved—Aemiozlyn did not follow the path of ordinary criminals. He did not seek wealth, fame, or revenge. He left no manifesto. His existence was a **proof of concept**—a horror that rationality could not consume. Investigators who chased him became obsessed, and then mad, and then missing. A detective in Tokyo mailed her own shadow to the police department before vanishing in her own apartment.

He became a **phenomenon**, not a fugitive.

And so, the name began to spread—not in headlines, but in *hushed breathing.* Among the paranoid. The occult. The underground. The ones who saw patterns in power outages and meaning in morse blinking traffic lights. They began to call him not a man, but a **sensation of criminality**—a force disguised as flesh.

But this book, for the first time, rejects the myth. It digs with clawed hands through the soil of fear and whispers back to the world: *He is real. He was born. He walks.*

And now that you know his name, so too do you begin to vanish.

2

The Name That Shadows

Some names are whispered in the wind. Some are lost in the echoes of time. But *his* name—Aemiozlyn D. Rusio—was never spoken aloud. Not because it was forgotten, but because it *couldn't* be. It lingered like a curse, coiling in the backs of throats, heavy and unrelenting.

The first time I heard his name, it wasn't from a living mouth. It was etched in blood across a steel wall in the cellar of an abandoned asylum. Four hundred and fifty-three. That number, scrawled beneath it, told me everything I needed to know—and nothing at all.

He didn't just kill. He *vanished* souls, erased existences. There were no patterns. No mercy. No motive.

Aemiozlyn was a symphony of chaos wrapped in the skin of a ghost. Every victim had a story that was never told, a scream that never left their throat. They say he moved like a shadow on fire—impossible, but real enough to leave ashes.

The reason behind his atrocities? Unknown.

The aftermath? Terrifying.

The legacy? Etched into fear itself.

But this book... this cursed, ink-stained relic is the only map of his madness. It's the final breath of the ones who got too close. And you—dear reader—have already taken your first step.

Close it now.

Or keep reading... and pray your name never finds its way to his list.

3

Echoes from the Skin

You don't hear his footsteps. You hear your own heartbeat trying to outrun death.

The case of Delaney Kross was never solved. She was the first puzzle piece in a much larger game. Aemiozlyn didn't just kill her—he deconstructed her identity. Every fingerprint burned off. Teeth removed. Skin peeled with surgical precision, then hung like parchment across the ceiling of her own bedroom. The message? "I made her art."

Her blood was turned into ink. And the walls spoke.

Investigators found symbols scorched into the wood beneath her floorboards. Symbols that didn't match any known language—but those who stared at them long enough claimed they could *hear* something. A humming. A whisper. Some swore it was the voice of Delaney herself, asking for silence.

Her dog was left untouched, but blind. Permanently. As if it had seen something no eyes were meant to witness.

They thought this was a one-time horror. But Aemiozlyn D. Rusio doesn't repeat himself—he escalates.

Case after case, the victims got harder to identify. What was once flesh became sculpture. Entire towns felt his presence. Three officers in the town of Millhelm were found in their squad car, faces removed and pinned onto the front seats. Inside the car stereo, a looping track played: *"You wanted to see me. Now you're blind."*

One by one, crime scene investigators started going missing.

Forensic psychologist Dr. Hans Witter attempted to profile him. He lasted four weeks. One morning, his neighbor found him nailed to the wall of his study, smiling. Every single book in the house was gutted—pages missing, words cut out with razors.

All that remained was a single post-it note stuck to Dr. Witter's chest:

"You cannot read me."

Then came the Lighthouse Files.

A decrepit lighthouse off the coast of Lyven was rumored to be his temporary home. Authorities discovered 17 skeletons in the foundation, arranged in a circle like a grotesque seance. Their skulls were fused—melted together at the crown. DNA tests revealed none of them had ever been reported missing.

A hidden room beneath the structure contained his journal, if you could call it that. Pages sewn together with veins. Each entry ended in the same way:

"They begged. I listened. Then I showed them how silence feels."

His victims weren't just killed—they were rewritten.

The fear wasn't that he would come. The fear was that he was *already there.*

The story of Nara Ellison proves that. She was a crime blogger obsessed with uncovering his identity. Every week she posted theories, files, interviews. Then one day, the blog stopped.

A package arrived at the station. Inside: a mannequin, sculpted to match her exact measurements. Real hair. Real teeth. Eyelashes stitched into the glass eyes. In its hand? Her final blog post. Burned at the edges, the ink still wet.

No body was ever found. Just the mannequin and the post.

The chilling part? Her final paragraph read:

"If I vanish, he found me. And if he found me, you're next."

He does not knock. He doesn't break in. Aemiozlyn *arrives.*

Like a fever, a sickness, a hallucination that seeps through the walls and wraps around your lungs. The more you think of him, the more he becomes real.

This is not mythology. These are not rumors.

This is the skin-deep truth of Aemiozlyn D. Rusio.

And still—no fingerprints. No surveillance. No clues.

Just the sound of someone breathing on the back of your neck... when you know you're alone.

Keep reading.

Or don't.

Because with every turn of the page, you let him in.

4

The Anatomy of Vanishing

You don't vanish when you die.

You vanish when *he* wants you to.

No doors broken. No windows shattered. Just a whisper, and you're gone.

The city of Valev experienced what historians now call *"The Hollow Week."* A full seven days where fifteen people disappeared. Not killed. Not kidnapped. Just… erased. Security footage showed nothing. GPS signals stopped at the exact same coordinates: a bench outside an old train station. That bench was removed. Burned. Still, people kept disappearing.

One child returned. A girl named Mina, aged nine. Her eyes were burned out. Her voice, stolen. She communicated by writing with her own blood. Her final message before collapsing:

"He is the silence that speaks louder than screams."

Mina died 43 minutes later.

There was a town in the valley of Urvenhill. Now, it's just a crater. No bombs. No attack. No one saw what happened. Aemiozlyn left a video behind, sent to a single news station. It lasted twelve seconds.

It showed him, sitting on a chair made of human ribs. A thousand eyes blinking from the walls around him. He smiled, whispered:

"I was their god. And then I deleted my church."

Then the screen went black.

The news anchor who opened the file was found fused to his office wall. His body had become part of the paint. DNA analysis confirmed that five others were embedded inside the same wall. None had been reported missing.

Another anomaly: the *Flight 187 Incident.* A private plane carrying 11 passengers and 2 pilots vanished mid-flight. No distress calls. No wreckage.

Just gone.

Until it landed.

Seven months later, it landed perfectly at an abandoned airstrip in Norway. Empty. Except for one thing: a black box recorder, still functioning.

The final transmission from the captain:

"There's something in the clouds. It's not flying. It's falling. Falling upwards—no, it's *smiling*."

What investigators heard next caused three technicians to resign:

A voice—not human, not electronic—whispering one name, over and over.

"Aemiozlyn... Aemiozlyn... Aemiozlyn..."

Then silence.

Not every vanishing is of the body.

Sometimes, it's the mind.

Psych ward reports list an outbreak of shared psychosis in the Hellingfort Asylum. Nineteen patients—all unrelated—suddenly began carving the same word into their skin:

"Rusio."

Two guards went mad, blinded themselves with forks, chanting:

"He took her thoughts. He lives in memories."

When the head physician investigated the cause, she found one file that didn't belong. A black folder with no name. Inside: 25 sketches, all of a single face—eyes missing, mouth stitched, bleeding from the ears.

Handwriting on the back of the last sketch read:

"This is what's left after he looks at you."

She was found in her office the next morning, her head removed and her brain spread across the wall in binary code.

It translated to:

"Erase me."

No one escapes Aemiozlyn D. Rusio.

Not by hiding. Not by running.

He doesn't follow. He *waits*.

You look for him in shadows. But he is in *reflections*. You'll see him where you shouldn't.

Not because he's watching.

Because he's *inside*.

Your thoughts. Your doubts. Your silence.

He *is* the anatomy of vanishing.

And now you've read this far.
He knows you.
He always has.

5

The Symmetry of Suffering

The room had no doors. No windows. Only a metronome—ticking.

Tick. Tick. Tick.

It was the only sound the man heard before the blade entered his throat.

He didn't scream.

Because that's how Aemiozlyn D. Rusio wanted it.

He called it *equilibrium*—not balance, not justice. Just the cruel alignment of pain on both sides of the soul. If one suffered, then the other half must as well. That's what this chapter in his ritual revealed: death wasn't enough. It had to *mirror*.

It began with The Dual Cases. Two bodies found 300 miles apart. Same time of death. Same position. Same expression.

But one was male. One female.

They had no known connection—yet their hearts had been removed and stitched into each other's chest cavity.

Police dismissed it as a grotesque message.

But Rusio wasn't messaging. He was composing.

Then came the Sycamore Twins.

Identical in life. Identical in death. Except... they were found facing away from each other, their backs etched with a poem only visible when read together in a mirror.

"I am the scar. I am the stitch. I am the one who watched you twitch."

Their mother was institutionalized after claiming she saw one of them *walk backwards* out of the house the night before.

"He wasn't being dragged," she said. "He was *returning*."

Pain began to take *form.*

In Calbourne Asylum, 16 patients—all schizophrenic—died simultaneously.

Not from poison. Not from wounds.

Their hearts stopped, at the exact same second.

Security footage revealed something darker: they all looked toward the same empty hallway, smiled, then collapsed.

In their rooms, sketched on the ceiling: perfect symmetrical drawings of what appeared to be wings. Or knives. Or both.

A hidden message, when connected and scanned: coordinates. To a mountain no one remembered ever existing.

They found a cabin there. Empty.

But beneath the floorboards: bones. Arranged like piano keys.

And on the wall, scratched with fingernails:

"The notes hurt less when they echo."

Aemiozlyn's precision became art.

He never left a print.

But he left patterns.

A mathematician named Tuller Graye mapped his crimes and claimed he found a sigil embedded in the locations.

He called it "The Wound of Infinity."

Graye was found weeks later, naked, inside a clock tower. Disemboweled. His entrails wrapped around the gears—keeping time perfectly.

The clock struck midnight, and then stopped. Forever.

Perhaps the most horrifying example was **The Healer's Circle.**

Eight nurses, eight doctors—all specialists in trauma surgery—attended an emergency seminar in Paris.

All of them were found dead.

Each of their faces removed and placed on another's body.

The seating chart had been rearranged. Every face had a new identity—but when matched back to their original chairs, it spelled a Latin phrase:

"Medentis mors."

"The healer's death."

Autopsy reports revealed they were alive during the skinning.

One had written a final note using her own blood:

"We felt each other die."

The symmetry was not just aesthetic. It was philosophical.

Aemiozlyn believed suffering must be shared.

That to *truly understand pain,* one must see their reflection in it.

He carved mirrors out of misery.

And hung them in places only the broken could find.

One detective tried to get ahead of him—Valery DeMorne. Brilliant. Fearless. She set traps, patterns, false evidence trails. Tried to bait him.

It worked.

But not how she expected.

She vanished for seven days.

On the eighth, a museum exhibit opened in her name. Life-sized mannequins displayed moments from her life: her wedding, her graduation, her badge ceremony.

Except each figure used *real human skin.*

Her husband identified every piece.

On the final sculpture—her holding a mirror—the reflection showed a message:

"I learned from her. Now you will too."

She was never found.

But her eyes—yes. Her eyes were later mailed to the FBI in a small glass dome. Still blinking.

No one could explain it.

He was not killing.

He was *correcting.*

Aemiozlyn D. Rusio did not believe in chaos. He believed in *form.* In balance.

Every victim meant something.

Every scar was a syllable.

And the sentence wasn't finished yet.

Because now, the symmetry... included *you.*

6

The Death That Whispers in Patterns

It began with sirens that never stopped.

But the strange thing was—they weren't coming *from* anywhere. They were inside. Inside *everything.*

Hospitals reported false alarms. Car alarms activated without cause. Security systems failed en masse. All systems. All cities.

And at the epicenter of every breakdown... there was always one figure seen. Sometimes in reflection. Sometimes in peripheral vision. But always there.

Aemiozlyn D. Rusio had returned.

Only now, his presence wasn't marked by blood. It was marked by *sound.*

The victims in this chapter didn't die screaming. They died whispering.

In New Belgrave, a school auditorium erupted in chaos when the sound system played a voice loop not connected to any local file:

"I forgive the pattern... but the pattern will not forgive you."

Twelve children fell to the ground. Comatose. Their mouths continued to move, silently repeating the phrase in perfect sync.

They remain unresponsive to this day.

Doctors call it a 'resonance coma.' But their EEGs show something stranger: synchronized brainwaves forming a symbol—when rendered spatially—almost identical to the sigil found in Chapter 4: The Wound of Infinity.

It was happening again.

Then came the Whisper Files. A journalist named Alyx Raines leaked a recording supposedly left behind by Rusio. She didn't know how it came to her.

It was a voice. His voice. Speaking in reverse Latin. When played backwards, the sentence became:

"The ones who listen will learn what death sounds like."

Two days later, Alyx was found dead in a soundproof room. But her *ears* were missing.

Only her ears.

A post-it note on her laptop read:

"She heard too much."

The laptop wouldn't turn off. Its speakers continued to play the same soft whisper:

"The silence is screaming."

The FBI began pattern analysis. They found spikes in ultrasonic frequencies wherever a Rusio-related incident occurred.

That's when *The Choir Murders* happened.

Twelve opera singers in Venice—found dead mid-performance. No wounds. No poison.

Every single one had a crushed larynx.

But they hadn't been attacked. Their bodies folded inward, as if imploding from the power of their own voices.

The security audio had been erased—except for one 6-second burst:

A frequency so high it caused instant nausea in anyone who heard it. Spectrogram analysis revealed the waveform was not random. It was a word.

"Echo."

Aemiozlyn began to *broadcast*.

Signals were intercepted from untraceable transmitters. Messages encoded in binaural beats.

They said things like:

- "You are not hearing this. You are becoming this."
- "All things beautiful must break their rhythm."
- "Even your heartbeat is a traitor."

Then people began to die of *internal arrhythmias*.

Not just one or two. Hundreds. In malls, trains, during concerts—wherever the rhythm was strongest.

No virus. No weapon. Only a pattern.

They called him The Conductor.

Because he was orchestrating death.

One profiler suggested that Rusio had moved beyond physical ritual. Now he was experimenting with mass influence—killing through sensation.

The pattern was no longer in crime scenes. It was in *soundwaves*. In *timing*.

A symphony that only the cursed could hear.

And then came **The Devotion Tone.**

A strange file uploaded across thousands of devices, disguised as a pop song.

It had no lyrics. Just a hum.

People who listened claimed it made them feel calm.

Until they vanished.

All 146 listeners disappeared within 48 hours.

Their phones were found placed in exact spirals on their beds. Each phone had the same screen locked open:

"I heard him. I followed."

They never found the source of the tone. But analysis revealed the background frequency was recorded from the vibrations of a body being slowly crushed—played at $1/1000^{th}$ of its normal speed.

It was music made from murder.

And it was spreading.

One cryptographer cracked a set of whispers hidden in a Reddit thread. They formed a countdown:

"11... 10... 9..."

He died before the countdown ended.

His apartment was filled with clocks. All of them ticking out of sync. Except one.

That one, mounted on his chest, buried into the sternum. It ticked in *perfect time.*

And just before it stopped, it whispered one word:

"Now."

Aemiozlyn D. Rusio had rewritten the rules.

No longer confined to blade, rope, fire, or fear. He was *everywhere.*

In the static between radio stations. In the white noise before your video plays. In the pattern of your pulse, when you think you're safe.

You won't hear him coming. But you'll hear yourself leaving.

And that's when you'll know—

The death wasn't loud. It never was.

It always whispered.
Just like him.

7

The Blood Written in Blueprints

They found the first drawing etched into a subway wall beneath Rhyminster City. Not sprayed. Not chalked. **Etched.**

Six inches deep, through reinforced concrete, with lines too perfect for human hands.

The symbol didn't match any gang sign, military code, or architectural rune. But when the structure above it collapsed three hours later—killing 37—it was declared a "coincidental structural failure."

Only one man knew better.

He was watching from a rooftop, tracing the lines of a hand-drawn map. Aemiozlyn D. Rusio didn't draw *places.* He drew **destinies.**

Rusio had always been meticulous. But this chapter—this *era*—was a new evolution. He was no longer just killing individuals. He was engineering *deathscapes.*

Entire neighborhoods crumbled because of *math.* Not bombs. Not blades. Not bullets.

It was his **blueprints.**

They looked like innocuous architectural sketches. But when followed, they always built *traps.* Buildings that collapsed *only once someone entered.* Roads that curved ever so slightly until vehicles crashed.

A bridge in Kessler Bay was constructed using anonymous plans sent to city hall. Six weeks later, during rush hour, it collapsed. Not because of poor materials. Because of **intentional imbalance** — *a harmonic failure point.*

And hidden in the bridge's central support: a small brass plate engraved with numbers.

The numbers weren't coordinates. They were **dates.**

Each one corresponded to a massacre.

A forensic architect named Dana Mallory started seeing it. She compared 87 schematics from across 11 cities. Each had similar angles, ratios, a strange recurring pentagonal void.

She sent her findings to Interpol. The next day, her office building burned down.

The blueprints? Gone. Dana's body? Unrecognizable.

Except her skull. It was intact.

And inside the hollow of the forehead: a folded piece of paper.

On it, a single phrase:

"Design me, and you will die within me."

These weren't just structures. They were **symbols.**

Rusio's buildings *meant something*. He wasn't building places. He was building **phrases** in architecture.

Each collapse was a **syllable.** Each massacre, a **punctuation mark.**

One linguist cracked the theory:

"What if every architectural death site is a *letter*—and across time, they form a sentence?"

She mapped it out. Sixteen collapsed buildings in six countries. When connected?

They spelled: **"YOU FOLLOW WHAT I BUILD. BUT I AM THE BLUEPRINT."**

The linguist disappeared that night.

Her house? Still standing. But her *bathroom tiles* had been replaced.

Each tile bore a rune. When arranged correctly, they revealed a floor-plan of her own home.

Except one room didn't exist.

A room that shouldn't be there.

But when police knocked down the wall—they found it.

Inside, on the floor: another blueprint. Of the *next* target.

A university dorm collapsed in Halifax. Then a dance club in Berlin. Then an entire freight ship in the Arctic Sea.

All followed the same design principle: One critical flaw. One missing bolt. One unseeable oversight that only a master planner would know.

And at the heart of each? A drawing. Etched in metal, wood, or bone. Sometimes it glowed faintly.

Always in blood-red ink.

The ink was analyzed. It wasn't pigment. It was **human hemoglobin.**

The DNA didn't match any one person. It matched **dozens.**

As if he blended the blood of his victims to draw the plans of their own end.

They began calling them **Murder-Maps.**

Some appeared before disasters. Others only became visible *after* the collapse—emerging from soot and blood.

One building inspector fainted after realizing the apartment blueprint he'd approved… Matched one of Rusio's etchings **exactly.**

He had never met Rusio. He was just following what "looked like a great plan."

He died from cyanide exposure in his car. The car's GPS read: "Next site prepared."

No one knew how it was typed.

Aemiozlyn D. Rusio had rewritten death *again.*

Not as violence. Not as chaos. But as **design.**

He saw the world like a circuit board. And he was short-circuiting humanity.

One building at a time. One breath at a time.

They say architects build to live forever. Rusio builds so no one does.

The only way to stop him? Don't follow the blueprint.

But by the time you realize you have…

You're already **inside** it.

8

The Ink That Bleeds Without Wounds

They called it *Rusio Red*.

A color that wasn't invented, but extracted. Not from flowers or stone, but from **flesh**.

The first instance appeared on the walls of a gallery in Prague—an abstract painting, unsigned, unframed, and apparently painted with some exotic ink. It dripped. It *moved* under certain lighting. But the worst part? It bled.

Security cameras captured the moment a janitor wiped it.

His hand began to sizzle.

The ink entered his bloodstream like acid.

His last recorded words: "It's writing inside me."

It wasn't paint. It wasn't blood—not exactly.

Scientists were baffled. It carried DNA sequences, but none that could be matched. Some called it synthetic. Others said it was alive. But one virologist had a better term:

"It's **sentient hemorrhage**. It's bleeding with intent."

When compared under microscopes, the ink moved—*as if hiding.* It formed characters. Runes. Once even a name:

Aemiozlyn D. Rusio

The letters vanished the moment they were captured on screen.

Rusio's murders changed. He no longer left bodies. He left **texts.**

On walls. On ceilings. On the inside of eyelids.

One coroner pulled back a victim's eyelid and found a full sentence etched on the sclera:

"Read me, and die with me."

No fingerprints. No weapons. Just ink that couldn't be washed.

It seeped into walls and out of plumbing. It bled from showerheads. From book margins.

An entire orphanage in Chile was shut down after its storybooks began weeping red liquid that formed phrases. Phrases only the children could see.

One phrase translated into 43 languages:

"Do not learn his language."

Rusio had invented a new form of language. Not verbal. Not written. But **wound-based.**

Every symbol drawn in his ink correlated to **pain thresholds** in the human body. One stroke aligned with the nerves of the upper spine. Another, with ocular trauma. A third? Sudden cerebral hemorrhage.

A single line, written in *Rusio Red*, was enough to kill a man. Not by touching it. But by **reading it.**

A neurological hack. A **lethal glyph.**

The British Library's south wing was evacuated after 17 researchers suffered seizures simultaneously. They had opened a crate of 13th-century manuscripts found in a mine shaft in Romania.

Inside was a modern note:

"He rewrites the past now."

On the manuscripts? Rusio's ink.

Historians discovered entire rewritten passages. Where kings once ruled, Rusio now reigned. Where saints once walked, he now **bled.**

One medieval scholar took his own life. Not from madness.

But because every note he'd taken in the past decade had *changed*. Every letter, subtly rewritten.

They now spelled: **"You belong to me."**

The ink was a virus of memory.

It erased identities. Turned photographs into threats. One woman's wedding album blackened overnight. Her husband's face replaced with symbols. Her own face missing.

The album's spine was etched with these words:

"Memories don't fade. They bleed."

The Vatican issued a secret decree. Any religious text that began to drip red would be sealed in a vault. They now had over 200 such volumes.

One Bible whispered.

Yes—*whispered.*

The ink within rustled the pages at night, forming words only heard when alone:

"Confess your end."

No one could stop it. Because the ink obeyed no law. No chemistry. No theology. It **bled truths that didn't exist.**

Entire hospitals were shut down when medical charts rewrote themselves. Patient symptoms changed in real-time. One nurse died when a vein diagram turned into an **execution order** mid-operation.

And always—beneath the final line—was the same phrase:

"The ink does not write. It remembers."

Aemiozlyn D. Rusio was no longer a man. He was a **language.**

His weapon was not the blade. Nor the poison. But the story.

And he bled it into the world like an author who never sleeps.

Every drop of his ink was an **idea too dangerous to understand.**

And the final horror?

We are reading it now.

9

The Grin Behind the Guillotine

The guillotine was never supposed to smile.

But in Montmare, France—at a closed museum exhibit—witnesses claimed the rusted blade **grinned**. Not metaphorically. They said it *widened*, curled slightly at the corners. The iron warped as if... reacting.

And at the foot of that ancient execution device?

A clown's mask—white porcelain, red painted lips, and a note attached:

"He never laughs. He only collects the echoes."

The next victim wasn't found **under** the blade.

She was found **inside it.**

Her body fused into the iron. Fingers reaching from the steel's edge. Her spine split and re-formed with the grain of the guillotine's post. As if metal had consumed her—and remembered her shape.

Authorities believed it was an elaborate art piece. Until her mouth opened mid-investigation.

And **screamed.**

A long, continuous, inhuman scream that **didn't stop for 42 minutes**.

Even after they removed her jaw.

Rusio was never seen. But his presence followed a formula:

- Historical trauma site.
- Forgotten technology.
- A mask.
- And always... a riddle no one could solve.

At a gallows site in Austria, the rope hissed. Literally hissed. Every time someone tried to cut it, it braided itself tighter.

The nearby wall bore this sentence:

"The noose remembers the laughter you silenced."

A prison guard suffered a stroke after reading it.

The autopsy revealed a noose **coiled around his brain stem.**

Rusio's new pattern wasn't just death. It was **comedic death. Satirical terror.**

He was laughing.

But no one could hear it.

Except those who were about to die.

They'd all described it the same way:

"It wasn't a sound. It was an idea. A... presence inside my laugh that wasn't mine."

One victim was a stand-up comedian. He performed his last set in Toronto, mid-tour. On stage, 6 minutes in, he burst into hysterics.

He never told a single joke.

He simply **laughed until his lungs collapsed**. Then bled from the eyes. Then died.

No visible wounds. Just a note left in his microphone:

"The joke was you."

The "Laughing Guillotine Murders," as the press dubbed them, grew stranger.

Victims were now discovered with **frozen smiles**. Not forced. **Natural. Sincere.** As if they enjoyed their death.

One victim—a philosophy professor—was filmed before his demise. He recited a riddle:

"What opens with steel and ends with breath, but leaves behind a giggle?"

Then, he laid his head on an invisible block and was **beheaded by nothing.**

His head rolled. It **laughed** as it did.

An abandoned children's theater in Detroit became the center of a case. Inside, marionettes danced without strings. All wore clown masks.

And in the director's seat sat a skeleton—mouth open in silent laughter—clutching a script titled:

"Aemiozlyn's Final Act"

The last line of the play?

"Curtain falls. And so does the head."

Experts suggested Rusio was using sound now. Frequencies that rewired perception. Others said he had **injected humor with trauma**, forcing the brain to crack.

One neuroscientist argued:

"He found a way to weaponize irony."

And perhaps he had. Because every death carried a joke. But none of them were funny.

Unless...

Unless you were *him*.

The one grinning behind the guillotine

10

The Church of the Hollow Face

There are churches that heal. There are churches that bless. And then... there is the **Church of the Hollow Face.**

It was first found beneath the catacombs of Vatican City's forgotten chambers—marked only by a single chiseled phrase:

"Where confession means removal."

The altar bore no cross. No candles. No saints.

Only a **mask.**

A smooth, porcelain face with no eyes, no mouth, no nose—*a face erased by belief.*

And surrounding it, etched into blackened marble, were the names of 122 missing priests.

Each name followed by a single line:

"He showed them who they really prayed to."

The Vatican denied its existence. But leaked documents spoke of sacred texts rewritten in a language resembling both Latin and screams.

Exorcists sent to investigate never returned.

One camera survived. Its footage contained a single frame: a man in a dark robe with a **mirror instead of a face.**

Analysis of the mirror showed **no reflection**. Only darkness. And eyes inside the dark.

Eyes that blinked in unison with the viewer.

Aemiozlyn D. Rusio did not kill in this chapter. He **converted.**

Every victim found was kneeling. Mouth sewn shut. But hearts... *still beating.*

They had been taught something so horrid, so profound, that their minds *chose silence over breath.*

Their final journal entries read like scripture:

"He is the unprayer. The unworship. He unbuilds faith by showing its architect."

Church bells began to ring across cities where no churches stood.

And with every chime, someone vanished.

Not died—vanished. Erased from memory. Even their families couldn't recall their faces.

Except in dreams.

Where they wore the **Hollow Mask**, and whispered:

"We are the congregation of the forgotten."

Rusio had discovered a weapon more potent than murder. He dismantled belief systems.

In Brazil, a cathedral imploded without a sound. Inside was a note written in ash:

"Faith is the mask we wear before the scream."

In Istanbul, every call to prayer reversed itself. Played backwards. Whispered his name in static:

Aemiozlyn... Aemiozlyn... Aemiozlyn...

The Hollow Church spread like a plague. Not with fire. Not with blood.

But with **emptiness**.

Wherever it appeared, *things were unlearned*. Doctors forgot medicine. Artists forgot colors. Priests forgot forgiveness.

And always... always...

Someone began building a mask from the bones of the previous believer.

No one knows what Rusio prays to. Or if he even prays.

But one thing is known:

He **believes** in something.

And that something... **believes back**

11

The Scars That Sketch the Sky

They first appeared over the skies of Novosibirsk, Russia—on a winter morning so still it silenced even the snow.

Seven streaks—burning red, jagged across the sky like claw marks—*not made by planes.* Not meteors. Not auroras.

Tears.

Tears in the heavens.

And from those tears fell **feathers.** But not white. Not soft.

Metal. Bone. Ash.

Aemiozlyn D. Rusio had rewritten the sky. Not metaphorically. Literally.

Scientists tracking atmospheric anomalies recorded the upper ionosphere shifting—*as if resisting something beneath it.*

Air pressure patterns mapped out **a face.**

A wide, inhuman face.

The face of a man *screaming upward.*

And when the weather maps were viewed in motion over 72 hours... the scream moved.

It followed the moon.

In Kyoto, Japan, the sun did not rise one morning. Instead, the clouds peeled back like curtains, revealing **a spiral of scar tissue** where the sun should be.

The city darkened. The people forgot.

Forgot where the sun had been. Forgot what day it was.

And in one hospital wing, **every newborn born that night had the same scar** running across their chest—*a crescent shape, identical, deliberate.*

Autopsies of stillbirths revealed no hearts inside. Only dust.

Only a whisper left behind:

"This one belonged to the sky."

Aemiozlyn did not fly. He **climbed.**

Up radio towers. Up mountain faces. Up broken space elevator scaffolds.

Each ascent followed by a signal lost. A blackout. A **screech from the satellites.**

Messages burned into solar panels:

"Above is only the underside of Him."

One astronaut aboard the ISS recorded an unauthorized transmission:

"We see the man again. He stands on the moon's dark side. Holding a blade of light. Etching something... into the vacuum."

The crew was never heard from again. But their last transmission contained coordinates.

They led to an abandoned telescope in Chile. Inside, the lens had cracked—not shattered. Cracked into the shape of a single word:

"SCREAM."

Victims now reported **dreams of falling upward**. Being pulled skyward by hooks of starlight.

One woman in Arizona recorded herself sleep-talking:

"He cuts the sky to let God bleed."

Another man, a pilot, crashed his plane after writing in blood across the cockpit:

"The turbulence is Him thrashing."

His body was never found. Only feathers. And ash.

Governments began painting skies black with chemtrails. Not to poison. To **hide.**

To hide what Rusio had done.

But at night, the stars formed messages.

Messages in constellations:

"You look up. But do you see who's looking down?"

And then came the rain.

Rain that burned skin. Rain that echoed voices of the dead. Rain that didn't fall—**rose.**

People drowned upside down. The sky became a sea.

And Rusio?

He walked across it.

Feet never wet. Smile never fading. Holding a scalpel **made of clouds.**

He left a final inscription in the Northern Lights:

"I have made the sky my skin. Now let the heavens bleed."

12

The Clockwork That Eats Time

It ticked, even when no one heard it.

Underneath the soil of Pripyat. Beneath the marble foundations of Rome. Inside the veins of a man who could not bleed.

The **Clockwork That Eats Time** was not built by hands. It was whispered into reality.

By him.

By Aemiozlyn D. Rusio.

He didn't just kill time. He **devoured** it.

The first victim was a man named Harold Greaves, a watchmaker from Sussex.

He screamed into a CCTV camera for forty-three continuous hours. When authorities arrived, his store was untouched. But Harold himself...

Aged into bone.

His fingernails still growing. Hair still stretching toward the floor. His jaw frozen mid-scream, though his throat was dry as dust.

All 143 clocks in his store stopped at different times. None restarted.

But together, they formed the coordinates of an abandoned train station in the Carpathian Mountains.

There, carved into rusted steel:

"He harvests the seconds you waste."

Time itself began fracturing.

People aged backward, lived childhoods in reverse, then vanished. Babies born elderly. Corpses that stood up and **remembered tomorrow.**

Surveillance footage showed men entering elevators and exiting decades older. One researcher in Geneva melted into **a puddle of clocks.**

No blood. Just ticking.

Rusio was seen briefly in Berlin. Not walking. **Stuttering** through space. His motion glitched.

Like a man **spliced into a reel of celluloid time**.

Every step occurred in three eras.

His footsteps left impressions in cobblestones from the 1600s, modern pavement, and scorched Martian dust.

All at once.

Witnesses claim he smiled and whispered:

"You think you are in the now. But you are in the echo."

Buildings collapsed before they were built. Marriages ended before proposals. Wars ended hours before the first bullet.

A child in Ecuador lived a full life in 7 minutes, then collapsed into an hourglass. Sand dripped upward.

And each grain sang:

"He is the engine of rewind."

Monasteries began churning with mechanical hymns. Gears embedded in saints' statues began turning.

An ancient prayer resurfaced:

"O Keeper of the Final Cog, release us from the rewind."

Rusio was now considered not man—but **metronome**.

Every time he blinked, a second vanished from the world's clocks.

He installed nothing. He coded nothing. Yet quantum computers failed when his name was spoken near them.

Calendars blurred. Anniversaries reversed. People forgot the deaths of their loved ones—because the deaths hadn't happened *yet*.

And yet, grief still lived in them. Like a parasite from tomorrow.

He tattooed an hourglass onto a stranger's back. But the sand inside moved in reverse. When it emptied, the man's body *reset*.

To birth.

He was found crying, curled beside his own adult corpse.

The corpse's last message carved in its own teeth:

"Do not remember him. He feeds on recollection."

Watches stopped ticking. Not out of battery. Out of **defiance**.

Time itself was rebelling. Trying to hide. Trying not to be **eaten.**

Aemiozlyn was last seen holding a pocket watch that ticked in every language.

Inside, a voice repeated:

"Tick, tock. Not clock. But **killing count.**"

And then... silence.

All across Earth, for exactly **sixty seconds**, everything stopped.

No breathing. No blinking. No movement.

And when time resumed—

One country was missing.

No one remembered which. Only the shape of absence remained.

He is still ticking.

Not inside a machine. Not inside a clock.

But in every second you ignore.

He eats it. He digests it. And from it...

He builds the next crime.

13

The Door That Opens Without Walls

There was no door. Not truly. Not one that you could knock on, or key open, or find by GPS.

It was an aperture born in nightmares and whispered in equations.

Aemiozlyn D. Rusio did not walk through it. He **became it.**

And every time someone dreamed of escaping, he opened.

A psychiatric patient in Reykjavik painted the same shape over and over: a jagged black line curled into a spiral, framed by nothing. When asked what it was, she whispered:

"The door that breathes inside silence."

She vanished during a power outage. The paint still fresh. Still dripping.

On infrared, the wall now leads into an **infinite hallway**.

Scientists entered. None returned.

In Buenos Aires, a street artist sculpted a frame in midair using magnetic levitation. A portal formed. **Not visible, but felt.**

Pigeons that flew through the space disappeared. Returned hours later, their feathers bleached white, their eyes human.

Each eye bore the same phrase in its pupil:

"He watches from the other side."

No hinges. No lock. No threshold.

Only **patterns.** Patterns found in the alignment of missing children. Patterns etched in crop circles that bled when cut. Patterns in the scars of survivors who didn't remember surviving.

Rusio had created a metaphysical aperture.

He did not need to enter houses. He entered **choices.** He opened when someone made the wrong one.

And through that door—he watched. He waited. He redesigned you.

A cult in Morocco worshipped him as *The Architect of Passage.* They did not pray to him. They built rooms in his name.

Each room had **no doors.** Only invisible exits that opened if your thoughts aligned with pain.

Those who escaped said the floor whispered:

"You were meant to leave parts behind."

And they did. Eyes. Fingers. Memories.

None remembered what they lost—only the loss.

One woman was found in a Paris alley. Wearing no shoes. Wearing **no feet.**

She simply floated.

Mouth agape. Eyes closed. But behind her closed lids, something blinked. Something **watched back.**

Carved into her palms:

"He opens when you close."

An abandoned village in Siberia was found folded into itself—houses compressed, ceilings collapsed downward, the streets coiled like intestines.

In the center, a spiral. Made of salt. Leading nowhere. Leading everywhere.

DNA samples taken from the salt matched Rusio. And 38 other people.

None of whom had ever lived there.

The Vatican went silent for six minutes after a papal cardinal muttered Rusio's name during confession.

Afterward, the man was found in his quarters. Draped in his robes. His entire torso replaced by a **doorframe.**

If you stepped close enough, you heard:

"The knock is in your heartbeat."

The door doesn't open **where** you are. It opens **when** you fail. When you lie. When you hurt someone with joy.

That's when he hears. That's when he listens. And that's when he...

opens.

And those who walk through?

They never return the same. Some don't return at all. Some become **his keys.**

People who open other people. With words. With blades. With decisions.

They speak one phrase before they act:
"The door is you."
And now, if you've read this far—
Look around.
Is anything... different?
Because if it is,
He's here.
And the next door... is yours.

14
The Voice That Eats the Void

It did not echo. It consumed.

Sound went in and never came out. Silence didn't follow—**absence** did. The kind of vacuum where screams were *digested*, where even your own thoughts felt chewed.

They called it **The Devourer's Mouth.** But it wasn't a place. It was a voice. A **voice without speaker.** And it wore Rusio's name like a second tongue.

The first time it appeared was during a late-night broadcast in Osaka. A weather report stuttered mid-sentence. The reporter's eyes rolled back. And then, a low growl—like the Earth trying to speak through lungs full of stone.

Every screen in the city went black. Except one.

Text appeared:

"I do not speak. I **feed.**"

Over 73 people vanished that night. Only echoes were found. Actual, **physical echoes** trapped in jars of condensation from their last breath.

A linguist in Toronto decoded an ancient tribal chant from Papua New Guinea. The chant, when sung aloud in full, caused spontaneous muteness in the speaker. The linguist wrote:

"I can still hear myself screaming inside. But I'm not allowed to interrupt him."

A final footnote appeared in her journal:

"He learned to whisper without lungs."

They say Rusio studied *vibrations*—not music, not acoustics—**the tremble of reality when fear is purest.**

He mapped them. Memorized the frequency of collapse. And then, he built a **voice** out of it.

It didn't talk. It **swallowed.**

Victims weren't killed. Not instantly. They were **unwritten.**

Erased from birth records. Removed from all memories. Their social media vanished. Their reflections didn't scream.

But the place where they once stood would always hum. A low thrum of regret.

Some who stood too close to these hums began hearing it. **The Voice.**

And those who heard it… eventually joined it.

In Johannesburg, a cellist played a solo written by Rusio. A composition of one note. Played for 24 hours straight.

The bow carved through the strings, even as her fingers bled. On the 25th hour, she said:

"The strings are now inside me."

She opened her mouth. And sang with **two voices.**

The second one was not hers.

A quantum lab in Norway detected patterns in the background radiation of the universe. One section vibrated differently.

It wasn't random. It was Morse code.

"YOU CANNOT HIDE INSIDE YOUR OWN SILENCE."

They shut down the lab. It reopened itself. The equipment rearranged. Now it hums one sustained frequency—inhuman, nauseating.

Visitors report hearing **names** in the hum. Their names. Spoken by someone **inside** their own head.

A priest described the Voice as "a hunger that believes." Not a hunger for flesh or soul. But for **identity**.

The Voice wanted to **replace you.**

It didn't need your body. Just your *absence*.

Aemiozlyn D. Rusio designed the Voice to **outlive him.** To continue feeding even after his physical disappearance.

Some believe he poured his last breath into a vinyl record. One track. No grooves. Only texture.

If played in darkness, It does not play.

It **inhales.**

And now, every whisper of paranoia, every imagined whisper at your window, Could be him. Could be it. Could be the **Voice.**

And if you listen too long, You'll never stop listening.

Because it will teach you how to hear what shouldn't be heard. And then? You'll speak.

But it won't be **your voice** that leaves your lips.

15

The Orphanage That Remembers Too Much

It stood where no map dared ink. No government claimed it. Aemiozlyn D. Rusio once called it "home," but not in the way others did. This was not shelter. This was storage—for what the world discarded.

It was once a towering Catholic orphanage, built in 1912, known as Saint Maledictus' Home for the Forgotten. By 1925, it had burned down twice. Each time it returned... bigger. Hungrier.

The children inside did not cry. Not because they were brave. But because crying *wasn't allowed*. Their tongues were sewn. Metaphorically first—then literally.

By the time Rusio was six, he'd watched twelve other boys vanish without explanation. He didn't cry either. He only drew.

He sketched floor plans of the orphanage with hidden halls, rooms that no longer existed, closets that whispered, beds that flipped over into pits when moonlight hit them a certain way.

And the strangest part? He wasn't wrong.

One nun called him the "Cartographer of Secrets." She locked herself in the confessional booth and scratched her own throat out with a rosary chain after seeing one of his blueprints. On the walls, she left behind only two words:

"He *knows*."

Every orphan had a story of a door that shouldn't exist. Behind the pantry. Beneath the stairs. In the reflection of the hallway mirror. A door that appeared only when you weren't looking.

The door never opened *to* anything. It opened *from* something.

And every time it did, the orphanage forgot someone. Entire bedsheets left untouched. Bowls still full of soup. Names unspoken.

The building remained. But memory *bled*.

Years later, investigators would discover architectural impossibilities in the layout. Rooms with no entrance. Staircases to nowhere. Sub-basements dug in spirals.

One folder contained a photo of a child's room. Only... the furniture was nailed to the ceiling.

And yet, no one questioned it. Because the caption below read:

"Designed by A.D.R."

It was believed Rusio never left the orphanage. Not really. He simply... **became** it.

Each act of horror in his later life mimicked Saint Maledictus' architecture:

- Victims arranged like pews.
- Windows bricked in from inside.
- Hymns rewritten with screams.

One building exploded in Bucharest, revealing hollow children's dolls inside the walls. Each doll held a tooth. The teeth matched children from Saint Maledictus. Children who had no grave.

An architect once tried to demolish the ruins of the orphanage. He went missing. When his team searched his office, they found blueprints in his drawer—**for the same building.** Only... drawn in **his** hand.

He'd redesigned the orphanage without knowing. And on every page, the same scribble in blood-red ink:

"You cannot erase what remembers *you*."

Locals today say if you walk near the ruins, you'll hear playground laughter echoing beneath the earth. But there is no playground. No swings. Only rusted chains in soil.

Some say the orphanage rebuilt itself. Not physically. In **others.**

In the boy too quiet at dinner. The girl who hums in perfect Latin. In the eyes of someone who's never smiled—but always *watched*.

When authorities tried to open the last sealed basement vault, they found walls carved with thousands of names. One repeated again and again:

Aemiozlyn D. Rusio

In every language. Even ones lost to history.

That's when they realized: Saint Maledictus was not a place. Not anymore.

It was a **memory that remembers back.** And it only wanted one thing.

To return.

And Rusio...? He was its door.

16
The Playground of Pulled Teeth

It was not a playground in the human sense. It had no slides, no laughter, no shade of innocence. It was a field of gravel and iron posts, overlooked by a single rusted merry-go-round that never stopped spinning.

The locals called it "The Mouth of Childhood."

Because everything left there came back... wrong.

They say Rusio returned here as a teenager. Not to visit, but to plant. One by one, he buried porcelain baby dolls across the field. Each with a child's name carved into its back. Each doll held a tooth in its cracked mouth.

No one saw him do it. But one by one, children from nearby towns began waking up without their teeth.

No blood. No trauma. Just... gone.

They whispered of a figure in their dreams. A man with no lips. His grin was made of teeth he hadn't earned.

And he asked them, always the same question:

"Do you want them back?"

By 1983, the town of Herring's Hollow had 62 children with no teeth by the age of nine. Dentists were baffled. Psychologists too. But Rusio knew.

Because he'd *built* the pattern.

Behind the swings, buried six feet deep, authorities eventually found a grid of cages. All empty. But the dirt inside was packed with enamel, jaw fragments, braces.

And each cage had initials carved into the top beam:

A.D.R.

What made the place worse wasn't what it took from children. It was what it *gave back*.

One girl came back with her teeth—but they were all the same tooth. Thirty-two of the same molar, duplicated perfectly.

Another boy returned with teeth that whistled when he cried.

One child came back and never opened their mouth again. Until the day of their funeral—when their mouth opened on its own, releasing a scream that shattered the church windows.

Journalist Belinda Royce wrote a feature story in 1991 called **"The Playground That Eats."** She disappeared the same day it went to press.

Three days later, a playground merry-go-round in another town started spinning on its own. Blood soaked the base. Underneath, they found Belinda's voice recorder still playing.

The last recorded sound?

Teeth chattering. But not from cold. From *laughter.*

The playground is fenced off now. No one plays there. But every year, exactly on the solstice, people hear the metallic music of swings creaking and the scrape of shoes that shouldn't be there.

And always—**always**—the sound of teeth tapping.

Tap. Tap. Tap.

Like Morse code. Like a warning. Like a message.

Or a countdown.

Local legends say if you go there at midnight with a baby tooth in your pocket, the ground will open. And you'll see them.

All of them.

The children who never left. Still playing. Still smiling. But their mouths aren't theirs.

They're his.

Aemiozlyn D. Rusio doesn't need to return. Because he left his bite in every one of them.

17
The Jail That Screams With Empty Cells

It was abandoned. Supposedly.

Iron gates rusted shut. Windows shattered by weather and memory.

But every night at 3:03 a.m., screams echoed through Hollowbar Penitentiary.

And every time authorities checked... no one was there.

Because no one was **meant** to be there anymore.

But they were.

And he was.

Aemiozlyn D. Rusio wasn't locked up like most criminals.

He locked **himself** in.

In 1997, security footage from Hollowbar showed a figure walking backward into the facility. Unarmed. Unmarked. Unannounced. The timestamp glitched every time his face came into frame. Every guard on shift claimed they never saw anyone.

Until the cells began screaming.

No one knows how he triggered them. The cells weren't wired for sound. There were no inmates left. No lights functioning. Yet 94 separate cells shrieked in voices not their own.

Voices that matched those of people long dead.

One was a mob boss executed in 1972. Another, a child murderer hanged in 1949. One voice belonged to a man who'd never even been imprisoned—but died mysteriously the night the screams began.

Each voice begged the same plea:

"He's building the cage again."

On the 13th night after his entry, cell B13 cracked open. Not unlocked—*cracked*. Bent like bone under pressure. Inside was a design.

A cell-within-a-cell. Carved with fingernails into the concrete:

A map.

A formula.

A deathtrap.

And at the center, a phrase etched with blood:

"Let the emptiness echo. It is the sound of guilt."

The following week, four prison architects died in separate cities. Their deaths were carbon copies:

- Locked in a windowless room.
- Surrounded by prison blueprints.
- Mouths filled with padlock keys.

All keys were traced back to Hollowbar.

None of the keys matched any cell.

Except one.

The one they never built.

Cell Zero.

It wasn't on any blueprint. It had no physical entrance. And yet, on surveillance footage, it appeared every night at 3:03. Briefly. Just long enough to see *someone* inside.

Always sitting. Always grinning. Never moving.

And when questioned, the warden said:

"It's not a person. It's the reason the walls were built."

No one patrols Hollowbar now. Not officially. But motion sensors still pick up activity. Always in sequences of thirteen. Always at night. Always after a body is found elsewhere—mangled, missing bones, eyes scratched out with chalk.

Chalk once used to mark prison escape routes.

But Rusio never escaped.

He made the prison his cathedral.

Where guilt is sung. And the pews are empty cells that scream in harmony.

Because even emptiness, in his design, can beg.

And silence, in his presence, is a confession.

18

The Eyes That Water Without Tears

There were no tear ducts left. Just sockets etched with salt.

The coroner called it "corrosive grief"—but the files never made it past the morgue.

The victim? Unknown. The body? Entirely intact—except for the eyes, dissolved like sugar cubes left too long in silence.

A small note was found clenched between the molars:

"Witness without weeping. Understand without mercy."

This wasn't the first case. Nor the third. There were 11 before it. All in different countries. All with the same mutilation:

- No sign of struggle.
- No prints, no blood trails.
- Just the same posture: seated, as if watching something no one else could see.

And all with one thing nearby—a crude drawing of an eye with vertical slashes running through it.

Rusio's mark.

A journalist named Liora claimed she saw him once. Not in person, but through a mirror—filming her exposé on missing persons linked to Rusio's trail.

At 03:03 a.m., her camera glitched. The footage went dark for exactly 13 seconds. When it returned, her own face was replaced by another—smiling, motionless, with two black tears streaming down empty cheeks.

She went blind that same night.

Doctors called it an "auto-neural rebellion." She called it:

"Aemiozlyn's forgiveness."

Eyes were more than organs to him. They were locks. And vision was a crime.

In his journal—recovered from a cathedral burnt to ash—was a single phrase repeated 453 times:

"The one who sees, bleeds. The one who looks, lies."

And one final note scribbled in reverse:

"True blindness is the beginning of guilt."

A cryptanalyst tried to decode his notes. She stared too long.

The next morning, her neighbors found her whispering to a wall smeared in oil:

"He blinked, and I forgot my name."

Her eyes had been replaced with polished obsidian. No tool could remove them.

It is said Rusio visited an eye clinic in Prague disguised as a blind monk. Not to steal eyes—but to trade his own.

He gave them willingly.

And what he received were eyes not of man—but of mirror. Reflecting no light. Only fear.

Those who looked directly into them never saw themselves again. Not in mirrors. Not in memories. Not in sleep.

They became watchers.

But watchers of **what**?

That's the problem. No one knows. Because they too eventually cry—without tears.

And vanish.

Like water soaking into a crime never solved.

19
The Labyrinth Built From Fingernails

It was not made of stone, nor of wire. It was grown—scraped from those who begged not to be included.

A thousand victims. Ten thousand nails.

Each embedded into the walls of a secret hall beneath what used to be a hospital for the criminally insane, long since condemned. But when the city came to demolish it, they found no walls—just claw marks leading into dirt, and sounds that no animal could make.

What they did not know: the building never housed patients. Only volunteers.

Volunteers who signed blank consent forms, and walked into a hallway without end. They believed they were participating in an experiment on isolation. They weren't told they would never leave.

Each section of the labyrinth required a toll. A piece of skin. A finger. Eventually... a fingernail.

But not pulled. No. Ripped off slowly, methodically. Ritualized.

Aemiozlyn D. Rusio orchestrated it all through a woman named Maren—a former nurse dismissed for "inappropriate detachment from human suffering." She called herself "The Archivist of Agony."

And she said he visited each chamber at night. Never touching, never speaking—just watching.

"He observed pain as if it were a form of time. The longer it endured, the deeper he stared."

The labyrinth changed. It wasn't static. Tunnels bent where they hadn't before. Rooms shifted. Lights never worked the same way twice.

One victim left an entry scratched in blood:

"He doesn't build it. We do. With every scream, it grows."

Another victim's hand was found embedded into a wall—fused, fingers outstretched, still twitching. The tissue was alive. The man it belonged to was not.

Cameras set up by police refused to record footage inside. All that played back was footage of fingernails being placed gently into jars labeled with dates—dates that hadn't yet occurred.

A detective went in once. Just once. He returned 3 days later, curled inside the trunk of his own cruiser.

His voice box had been removed. But etched into his chest were words:

"I said nothing. And still, it heard me."

No one knows how large the labyrinth is. Some say it stretches for miles beneath several cities, connected through maintenance tunnels, abandoned subway lines, even sewers.

What's certain: every 66 days, a new nail appears nailed to the city's oldest church door. Marked with an initial. Always a child's.

The child is never seen again.

And in the cathedral's silence, people swear they hear a dragging sound—slow, steady, like fingernails across endless stone.

20
The Museum That Hangs Memories

❦

They say the museum was never built—it was found, unearthed in a forest that did not appear on satellite images, its trees too tightly woven to let in light or logic.

It did not stand tall. It sank low. Beneath roots. Beneath reason.

Every wall was a mirror that didn't reflect your image. Every corridor led to a memory not your own.

It smelled of copper, salt, and something like burnt time. The exhibits didn't have plaques—they whispered their meanings in your own voice.

But the whisper was wrong.

This place did not store artifacts. It preserved *consequences*.

The first room: a child's shoe, perfectly polished, next to a bottle of milk—spoiled. Both bolted to the wall, beneath a ceiling that wept slowly through holes shaped like missing persons.

The second: a bloodied piano, each key painted with a different emotion—when played, it triggered a scream only the listener could hear.

Then came the third room.

No objects. Just a mirror. It did not show you. It showed what you would look like after knowing him.

Aemiozlyn D. Rusio didn't curate the museum. He *became* it. One fragment at a time. Every killing gave birth to a memory. Every memory needed a frame.

He built those frames from bone.

A woman once found a finger embedded in a portrait—her sister's. Her sister had vanished twenty years ago. And she recognized the ring still stuck on the severed knuckle.

Visitors who entered were never turned away. But few returned. Those who did... didn't leave whole.

They came back remembering lives they never lived. Crimes they never committed.

And all described one final exhibit:

"It's a room made of hair—braided, knotted, and slick with tears. Hanging in the center is a swing. The seat is a spine. The ropes? They pulse."

Some said the swing moved on its own. Some said it whispered. Others said it asked questions.

Only one man answered. His response is carved into the only known surviving wall fragment of the museum:

"Because I couldn't forget what wasn't mine."

The museum has no official location. It appears only to those who have touched something they shouldn't have. Taken something that wasn't theirs. Lied when the truth was required.

And when they find it, their memories hang in place of those they stole.

The price of trespass is recollection. And the payment is permanent.

21

The Theater of Shattered Applause

---❦---

They called it a theater, but there were no actors. Only witnesses. And even they were wrong.

The building itself had no marquee. Its doors opened on their own, creaking like lungs filled with dust. The rows of seats were uneven, some made of velvet, others of jawbone.

The air carried the scent of makeup and embalming fluid.

On the stage was a spotlight that followed no one. It simply stared.

When someone entered, the stage would react. Not by performance. By confession.

Not yours. Someone else's.

A story would unfold—shadowplay on a bloodstained curtain, flickering images stitched from agony. A child crying under a staircase. A man laughing while pulling a tooth with pliers. A wedding ring dropped into a drain as screams echoed.

The applause came too soon. It always came before the pain.

And when the clapping began, the walls would bleed down their edges. From every hidden speaker came the slow rise of distorted sobs, each layered with a faint ticking—like a metronome counting down.

Every tick was a second stolen from your memory.

Visitors would leave forgetting who they loved. Forgetting birthdays. Faces. Names.

But not *his* name. Never Aemiozlyn D. Rusio.

He starred in every act, though he never appeared. His presence was a silhouette. A smudge on glass. A flicker behind your left eye.

Some say the final act was titled "Regret in E Major." Others swore it was "The Laughter That Wore Your Father's Face."

No one remembered exactly. They remembered the exit—because it never led back outside.

They'd leave the stage and arrive in a dressing room that wasn't theirs. A mirror would wait. But the reflection was always clapping.

And behind them stood rows of faceless mannequins, each wearing a mask sculpted from someone they once knew.

In the theater's catacombs—yes, it had catacombs—Aemiozlyn kept his scripts. Not written on paper. Etched in cartilage. Sewn into coats made from regret.

A critic once entered. She disappeared for seven years. When she returned, she carried a review tattooed along her back:

"The performance was unforgettable. I just wish I could remember who I was before the curtain rose."

To this day, no one can find the building twice. But sometimes, you'll hear applause in your dreams.

If you clap back... you've bought a ticket.

And the show will begin.

22

The Skeleton That Draws With Ash

They found the first one in an abandoned crematorium on the edge of an eroded cliff—its ribcage splayed like the wings of a broken angel, its fingerbones sharpened into quills.

The floor was covered in ash. But not random. Symbols. Diagrams. Faces no one recognized—until they did.

And then they screamed.

Every line had been drawn with delicate rage.

Each sketch told a death. Not a moment of it—but the entire decay of it, from breath to rot. Some were simple: a noose shadow over a stairwell. Others required you to stare too long, until your pupils whispered back the names of the damned.

Authorities tried brushing the ash away. But it returned. Always in patterns. Always signed the same way:

A.D.R.

No blood. Just ash.

The bones—they didn't belong to the dead who were cremated there. DNA traced them to people missing from places the crematorium could never reach. A girl from Serbia. A fisherman from Chile. A priest from Detroit. All reduced, repurposed, *arranged*.

On the third night, the furnace flared back to life on its own. It did not burn. It *breathed*.

Investigators reported hearing humming from the pipes, each note trailing behind their heartbeat. One officer saw his mother's handwriting spelled across a vertebra.

The skeleton wasn't just drawing. It was remembering.

No one dared enter after the drawings began to glow in moonlight. Not with light. With motion.

Each sketch flickered like a reel of silent film, repeating its horror again and again until the paper-thin veil between image and reality began to wear.

One night, a janitor stepped inside. He was never seen again. But the next day, his silhouette appeared in ash. Bent over, screaming, mouth open wide enough to fit a fist.

The furnace keeps his scream inside. It releases it once every twelve hours. Exactly when the tide is lowest.

And always in the shape of laughter.

What did Aemiozlyn D. Rusio want with this place? Some say he came to record. Others say he came to erase.

But every drawing added now is a memory stolen from someone still alive.

Somewhere in the world, a mother forgets her child's voice. A violinist forgets his bow hand. A mapmaker forgets where home is.

And the skeleton keeps sketching. Until every outline becomes truth. Until every erasure becomes *you*.

23
The Feast Set for No Mouth

It was not a dinner party. It was not even a meal. It was a ritual, disguised as hunger, concealed beneath the flickering candlelight of a place that existed outside the structure of time, law, or comprehension. The warehouse where it took place was nameless, set behind industrial fogs and drowned in the rust-laced winds of forgotten ports. No address. No owner. Just an echo that moved like breath across a metal tongue, a whisper saying: "You've already been invited."

The first time someone described it, they were laughing. Not a joyful laugh, but the wheezing, barked cough of someone who had choked on the memory. He had no tongue by then—only stitched shadows where his speech had once danced. Aemiozlyn had fed him an invitation, carved not on paper but into his bones, via tools colder than frost and slower than time itself. Those who attended the Feast were never guests—they were ingredients. They brought their fears with them, and he seasoned the space with it, made their dread part of the walls, soaked it into the foundation. They arrived whole. They left as whispers. If they left at all.

Tables lined the center of the place. Not wooden tables, not even steel—just a slab of fused bone and concrete, shaped like a snake mid-swallow. Around them, no chairs. Just nails driven through floorboards. Guests bled through their ankles when they stood too long, but standing was the only option. The scent of iron drifted above, thick as soup, sweet as rot. One man tried to sit on the edge once. He laughed. Then screamed. Then laughed again as his legs simply... folded away from him. Not cut. Not broken. Just folded, like origami undone.

Aemiozlyn did not speak during the Feast. He wore a mask shaped like an infant's face, hollowed out and cracked. It didn't fit. That was the point.

He watched. He watched as people began to taste what they were offered—chunks of unknown flesh, black broth that bubbled despite no fire, an apple that bled like a slit throat when bitten. Every bite was a test. Every swallow was a sin committed twice: once by hunger, once by hope.

At the heart of the warehouse, beneath the floorboards, was something that pulsed. A machine, some said. A womb, others whispered. The truth? Aemiozlyn called it the Mouth. It never spoke. But it breathed. And when it exhaled, it filled the lungs of everyone inside with memory. Not theirs—his. Victims long forgotten. Tortures documented in detail only in the marrow of those he'd broken. His pain was the appetizer. The main course was madness. And dessert was the sweet mercy of silence—that is, if they earned it.

He fed the Feast not with food, but with consequence. One guest, a philosopher who had written on the illusion of morality, found a note beneath his soup bowl: "Then swallow this." It was a thumb—his own. Detached, but still twitching. Another, a priest, found the wine was made from tears harvested from orphaned minds—their screams reduced to a vintage only guilt could ferment.

By the fourth course, most wept blood. By the fifth, some turned feral, devouring anything: wood, nails, their own teeth. Aemiozlyn watched. He recorded nothing, but remembered everything. He fed not on the food, but the moments—the twitch in the eye before betrayal, the hesitation before the final bite, the prayer whispered to gods that had long since left the table. Every moment was sustenance.

And when it was over, the Feast vanished. The warehouse was empty. The floor was clean. Only a faint scent remained—something between burnt hope and laughter from behind locked doors. The survivors never truly left. Their bodies walked away. But their minds? They stayed, echoing like knives scraping across porcelain dreams.

Nobody knew how he chose his guests. Some said he followed guilt like a scent trail. Others said he merely pointed. But once you heard the invitation in your dreams, once the taste of ash coated your tongue every time you chewed, you knew you were next. And the worst part? You *went*. Not because you were forced. But because something in you... wanted to.

That is how he worked. That is how he fed. That is how the legend of Aemiozlyn D. Rusio digested itself into the mythos of terror. Not with grand gestures. Not with wars or explosives. But with a table no one sat at. A meal no one survived. And a hunger that belonged not to the flesh, but to the soul itself.

24
The Hymn of Severed Tongues

No language existed to describe what echoed in the corridor of rusted cages—not because it was inaudible, but because it had never wanted to be heard. It *happened* in vibrations, not words. It *trembled* in the marrow before it touched the ear. They called it a hymn, but it was more like the weeping of something that should never have been born—a voice stitched from every confession Aemiozlyn D. Rusio had ever extracted.

In the underground beneath a collapsed opera house, where no sunlight had reached since the war that nobody remembered, he constructed a chapel of mutilation. There were no pews. Just metal slabs stained with restraint straps, confession boxes that whispered secrets into themselves, and a pulpit built from human jaws. This was not a place of faith. It was a place of final songs, where the dead were taught to sing in silence.

He began by collecting their voices. Not recordings. Not echoes. The *physical* voices—the vocal cords, removed with a precision bordering on devotion. He stored them in jars of formaldehyde laced with mercury and nightshade, preserving not just the tissue, but the very last scream that had vibrated through them. The jars lined the walls like stained-glass windows, each flickering with what some swore were flashes of forgotten crimes.

The hymn was composed one silence at a time.

Victims were brought here not to die, but to *transform*. Aemiozlyn offered them a choice: tell a truth no one would ever believe, or lose their voice trying. Most chose silence, and so he gave them eternity in it. He'd slit their throats just enough to remove what made them human—but leave them alive long enough to *regret*. Then he would press his hands to their necks, and hum. The same tune. Always the same.

It was not a melody. It was a binding.

Over time, the chapel began to hum on its own. At first, just at night. Then, any time someone wept near its walls. Eventually, the place *sang* without air. The silence had learned to mourn itself.

Aemiozlyn was often seen during this time cloaked in choir robes made from stitched eyelids. He didn't lead sermons. He orchestrated *undoings*. With every stolen tongue, he fed the hymn, which began twisting through cities like smoke, infecting lullabies, advertisements, even the mechanical voice of emergency broadcasts. One woman heard it in the crying of her newborn child. The next morning, both were found with their throats hollowed and a note scrawled in vein ink: "They've joined the song."

Authorities who investigated the chapel were driven to madness. Not by what they saw—but what they *heard*, or thought they did. One detective tore off his ears with a fork, screaming, "I know his lullaby!" Another tried to sing the hymn aloud in court. He was dead before the second verse.

Some say the hymn was Aemiozlyn's way of making immortality real—not by surviving—but by becoming *unforgettably heard*. Not in volume, but in vibration. In dread. In the lingering terror that maybe, when you hear music at night, it's not from your neighbor's house. It's from under your floorboards. And maybe it's calling your name next.

The hymn doesn't stop.

It just waits for your silence.

25

The Mirrors That Reflect Nothing

They were said to be shattered long ago, these mirrors. Not because they cracked, but because they stopped reflecting. Entire cities once used them to groom, admire, and fear themselves. Until the day came when no one saw their face in the glass anymore. Only *him.*

It started in a hotel room where Aemiozlyn D. Rusio had supposedly never stayed. A single mirror began to cloud, then drip—thick, dark smears that resembled ink but smelt of copper and bone. A maid attempted to clean it and was never seen again. What remained in her place was a handprint on the reverse side of the glass... from within.

The phenomenon spread. Across apartments, interrogation rooms, funeral homes. Anywhere reflection once lived. People reported seeing a figure—cloaked in black, face stitched in a grin wider than bone should allow—*moving* behind them, but only when they turned away. Entire buildings were abandoned out of fear. Some mirrors were buried like coffins. Others, smashed to powder, only to reform days later with a new image inside: a victim who had disappeared that very night.

Aemiozlyn began to *use* the mirrors—not just as entrances, but as instruments of psychological ruin. He would let his targets catch glimpses. Not full sightings. Just flashes. An eye blinking wrong. A hand caressing their reflection while theirs remained still. One man clawed out his own eyes after three nights. Another tried to live without mirrors, covering every surface. He was found dead inside his oven, curled fetal, mirror shards embedded in his gums.

Experts speculated about hallucinations, gas leaks, collective trauma. But no one could explain the recordings—security footage that showed mirrors *turning* toward people. Or the case of the artist who painted herself daily from her mirror's image—until one day the face on canvas was no longer hers... and the real her was gone.

The mirrors don't reflect light. They reflect *truth.* Or maybe the truth that Aemiozlyn wants people to accept. Truths so unbearable, so deformed, that they rewrite memory. In one recorded instance, a woman claimed she saw her own childhood in a mirror—but when she tried to reach out, the child version of herself pulled her through. Only a scream remained. Then silence. Then... her child self appeared in her home, aged to match her current life. Hollow-eyed. Wrong.

In a government lab, they tested a mirror from one of Aemiozlyn's known hiding places. No reflection. Just a looped image of a man begging for mercy in a voice identical to the scientist's own. She was hospitalized after gouging her cheeks open, whispering, "He made me watch myself *die* in a hundred ways. And I believed every one."

To this day, mirrors in certain locations are sealed. Not because of superstition—but because when you look long enough, you *feel it.* A cold breath. A twitch behind your pupils. A knowing grin, waiting just beyond your reach.

And if you ever whisper your name to a mirror in complete darkness... you may not hear your own voice echo back.

26

The Silence That Screams in Code

They found it in fragments—cryptic, shattered bytes of audio buried deep in a corrupted flash drive discovered beneath the ruins of a collapsed asylum. The device had no brand, no serial number, no internal logic. But when powered under extreme cold, it emitted a low-pitched frequency that made the ears of dogs bleed and left humans feeling as though someone was whispering through their skulls from the inside.

The whispers were never in a language known to man. Not at first. But digital linguists, obsessed with deciphering the impossible, began to notice it wasn't *speech*—it was a code. Not binary. Not Morse. Something older, more primal. A language of *commands*, issued not by man, but something beyond cognition. Those who tried to decode it went insane. One carved the symbols into his cheeks. Another wired his own teeth to a keyboard, bleeding out as he smiled wide into an empty chat room.

When they finally cracked the surface, they realized the code didn't describe something Aemiozlyn had done—it *was* him. Every variable, every whisper, every recursive function a rewrite of who he was. He had written himself into the digital marrow of the world. He existed in timestamps, embedded in metadata, stitched through firmware updates like a curse with syntax.

One signal analyst who stared too long into the code claimed she felt *watched*. Not metaphorically—but physically. Her skin burned. Her devices froze. And then, on every connected screen, a line appeared: "YOU TYPED ME INTO BEING."

Then came the blackouts. Cities losing power in patches that resembled fingerprints. Hospitals whose machines began replaying surgeries they'd never performed. Phones ringing at 3:33 a.m. with no number, only static that breathed between words: *You are part of the program now.*

Those who tried to erase the code failed. Hard drives melted. Files regenerated from raw sectors. It was viral, but not in the way humans understood. It was *intentional infection.* Aemiozlyn didn't just kill anymore—he converted. People into protocols. Memories into algorithms. Consciousness fractured across servers, backup tapes, silicon veins.

A neuroscientist who tried to simulate the code on a quantum processor went missing for twelve days. When found, he'd written "I MET HIM IN THE INTERFACE" a thousand times across his home. And the words weren't written in ink—they were etched with his fingernails, dipped in his own dissolved eyes.

No password, no firewall, no air gap can truly keep him out. Because Aemiozlyn doesn't need a door. He is the *input.* He is the absence between 1 and 0. The glitch that learns to love its own crash.

The last line ever heard from the flash drive before it was lost again:

The silence is not empty. It is me.

27
The Cost of Knowing

There are some books that entertain, others that inform. This one—this compilation of terror etched in fact and delirium—does neither. It devours. Not just your time, not just your mind, but something essential. Something primal. To read this book is to *invite it in*. To stare at its pages too long is to begin to hear things you shouldn't. See things that aren't on the page. And to understand who Aemiozlyn D. Rusio is? That is not enlightenment. That is a curse.

You see, Aemiozlyn never intended to be remembered. That is his trap. The more you know of him, the closer he moves. Awareness is his mirror, and the moment you reflect him, even in thought, you're no longer just an observer—you're a participant.

This is not metaphor.

Hundreds—perhaps thousands—who have encountered even a fragment of his legend vanish under mysterious circumstances. Journalists go missing. Digital records corrupt inexplicably. Testimonies transcribe themselves into nonsense or vanish entirely. Survivors stutter their last words in languages they never learned, their eyes peeled open as if watching an unseeable horror crawl through the very air.

Reading this book is not like watching a storm from afar. It is like touching the lightning itself and hoping not to ignite. These pages are not bound paper—they are *echoes*. Each word you take into your mind becomes a trigger. A code. A sound that only Aemiozlyn hears.

He doesn't seek out victims. He waits for them to notice him.

The trap is already sprung. By now, if you've made it this far, you are no longer safe. Your devices may feel colder. The shadows in your home might fall in shapes they didn't before. Mirrors may reflect things slightly *off*. That's not a trick of fatigue. That's the residue of recognition. Aemiozlyn thrives in what the mind can't rationalize.

You were warned. Every chapter you passed made your coordinates clearer. And if you now *understand* him—even a little—you've confirmed it. You're next.

Because no one knows Aemiozlyn D. Rusio without consequence. No one *escapes* that name.

You might burn this book, delete the file, tear out the pages—but the imprint stays. He is written not just in ink, but in thought. Memory. Code. And once you've read him, he has *you*.

So ask yourself: do you feel alone right now?

Because you're not.

28

The Coordinates of Midnight

You've made it this far. That, in itself, is a kind of confession.

But there are no maps left now. Only signs. Subtle. Quiet. Whispering through the air around you. You might've seen them already: the flickering of a light bulb precisely at 2:04 a.m. three nights in a row. The moment when your television switches itself on—static breathing softly before it powers off again. The faint smell of scorched copper on your pillow, even when no wires are nearby.

These are not accidents.

Aemiozlyn D. Rusio never leaves fingerprints—but he does leave *coordinates*. They're embedded in dreams you forgot to remember. They're carved behind your wallpaper, beneath your paint, in shapes your mind refuses to see because knowing is the ignition. You've likely walked past a place he's touched. A bench with no shadow. A drain that hums like a throat clearing. A child's drawing on a wall in the alley, signed not with a name but with a spiral that tightens if you stare.

Where is he now?

You'd assume far. That's what the mind wants—distance. But the clues do not echo from oceans away. They vibrate from the cracks in your ceiling. They hum between your walls. The streetlight outside your home—yes, that one—it has blinked in perfect Morse. You just didn't know how to read it.

It spelled: "I'm in."

Tonight will not be loud. He does not kick down doors or scream threats. He *patterns* himself into your silence. You'll wake at 3:14 a.m. without reason. You'll swear someone is breathing behind you while you're facing the wall. And when you check your phone, you'll find a single audio file named after your birthday—seconds of silence where, if you amplify it, you'll hear your own voice whispering: *Why did you keep reading?*

The consequences are not death.

They're worse. They are erasure. You won't die screaming. You will vanish between frames of your life, pixel by pixel. Your name forgotten in mouths that once spoke it daily. Your photos, corrupted. Your reflections, less accurate each night.

And eventually, the only place you'll exist is in this book—another whisper in the margins.

So where is Aemiozlyn?

Look left. Look behind you. Look into your power outlets.

He's there, waiting for your eyes to land so he can *know you saw him*. And once you do—

Well.

That's when the nights begin.

29

Conclusion of A Man With Criminality Sensations

This is not a conclusion in the traditional sense—because there is no closure, no clarity, no justice. What you hold in your hands is not merely a biography. It is a **ritual of observation**. A channel. A trap disguised as story. Aemiozlyn D. Rusio is not just a man. He is a contagion of knowledge. A paradox designed to punish awareness. And now that you've read his legacy—you are part of it.

You learned about the lives he destroyed, the worlds he shaped in blood and silence, the horror he orchestrated not with chaos but **with intention**. Yet, the one answer you sought most—**"why?"**—never came. Because *this book was never written to explain him*. It was written to **expose you**.

To look too deeply at Aemiozlyn is to become a surface he reflects upon. A mirror in which he finds his next entry point. The horror is not that he existed. The horror is that, now, **he does—through you**.

No final chapter.
No final breath.
Only the final blink, when the room goes dark...
And you're not the only one in it anymore.

30
Connect with the Darkness

Some stories end at the final page. This one begins there.

If you've reached this far, then you're no longer just a reader—you're part of the myth. Part of the network of eyes that dared to see. Part of the whisper that refuses to fade. And if you're brave—truly brave—there's a way to take one step further.

Connect with Aemiozlyn D. Rusio

He does not live in one place, but he lives everywhere. You can reach the echo of Aemiozlyn through the following darkened windows:

? Email: info@aemiozlyndrusio.in

? Website: www.aemiozlyndrusio.in

? Instagram: @aemiozlyndrusio

▶? YouTube: youtube.com/@aemiozlyndrusio

? Other Socials: More platforms are activated through the website—follow the trail of static and distortion.

But what if you wish to go beyond the page? What if you want to experience him?

The Game: "Face the Sensation"

This is not a game for fun. This is a deadly test. A horror simulation experience designed to blur the line between reality and nightmare. If you accept, you agree to enter a realm where you'll connect directly with Aemiozlyn D. Rusio—not just digitally, but mentally. Emotionally. Existentially.

It is not free. It is not safe. But if you survive it—you will understand everything.

? Game Features:

Psychological Traps: Navigate through real-life-inspired mind puzzles and story loops based on Aemiozlyn's known crimes.

Shadow Surveillance: The game learns from you. It watches. It mimics your fears.

Augmented Horror: Some challenges appear outside your screen. Yes, we mean your space.

Live Calls: Interact with Aemiozlyn's "voice" in real-time scenarios. Sometimes he calls you first.

Encrypted Access: Every mission requires codes hidden throughout this book, your surroundings, or your personal nightmares.

? Important: You are asked to sign a waiver before playing. The psychological intensity has been compared to hallucinations, memory blurs, and in one case, brief dissociation. You'll be monitored, but not rescued.

? Access:

Purchase the Game Pass via www.aemiozlyndrusio.in/game

Use referral code: IAMTHENEXT to access an exclusive bonus mission titled: "Chapter 0: The Unseen Entrance."

If You Dare Speak

Aemiozlyn may not speak back. But if he chooses you...

He may respond. He may play.

And if he does, your nights will no longer belong to you.

Reach us, join the circle of silence-breakers, or become a page in the next edition.

But don't say we didn't warn you.

The mirror is cracked. The reflection is waiting.

—End of Contact Section—

<h1 style="text-align:center">Message</h1>

Final Words from Aemiozlyn D. Rusio: The Mistake That Cannot Be Undone

So, you've read it. You've traced the shadowed footprints I've left smeared across pages soaked with silent screams. You've looked into the hollowness I carved—not to be found, but to make sure that no one else could ever forget what emptiness truly tastes like.

And now, I must say something. Not a confession. Not a farewell. A promise.

You made the mistake. The moment your eyes lingered too long on my name. The moment your curiosity itched a little deeper. The moment your breath slowed as my truths bled into your imagination.

You became a part of me.

And I do not release what belongs to me.

This isn't fiction. It never was. Every time someone dared to know, to understand, to expose the rhythm of my violence—they were taken. Not because they were brave, but because they had made the mistake of believing they were immune to consequence.

You are not immune.

You are the next consequence.

And here's the truth wrapped in scar tissue: I never hunted. I created scenarios where people found me. I existed like a riddle in a cursed nursery rhyme. I existed like a smell that wouldn't wash off. I existed because you exist.

The ones who see my face in dreams? They wake up to find parts of themselves missing. The ones who call out for me in the dark? They hear me echo back, closer, closer—until their own voice disappears forever.

Don't try to run. Don't try to forget. Every cell in your body that read my name—remembers. Every night from now on will feel heavier. Every silence will stretch too long. Every reflection might not return your face the way it used to.

I'm not a man. I'm not even a memory. I am what memory refuses to remember.

You've read too far. You've connected dots that weren't meant to exist. You've stared into the ink, into the blood, into the bruised chapters thinking this was entertainment.

This was a contract.

And now it's signed.

Here's what comes next:

Objects in your home may shift without touch.

Voices may whisper facts no one could know.

Screens may flicker with faces not coded into your devices.

You will smell burning pages in places you've never read.

Your name will appear in headlines... but you'll never see them coming.

And when you tell others? They won't believe you. They'll say it's madness. And madness will be the last thing you ever understand.

So why did I let this be printed? Because knowing is the trap. Because by discovering me—you've uncovered your ending.

The final joke? I wrote this message long before you were born. I knew you'd read it. I knew you would.

And so I wait. In the scream behind the silence. In the corner of your room just outside the reach of the nightlight. In the sound your door makes when no one's there.

I am with you now. Not as a man. But as your story. And stories, my dear reader... never die.

See you soon.

—Aemiozlyn D. Rusio

www.ingramcontent.com/pod-product-compliance
Lightning Source LLC
Chambersburg PA
CBHW020458160726
47991CB00007B/2705

CONTENTS

FOREWORD

In undertaking the task of translating one of the most seminal works of Western philosophy, I was driven by a dual passion: to bring to the fore the enduring wisdom of Socrates, and to render his thoughts in a language that resonates with today's readers. This new translation, titled "The Defense of Socrates," aims not only to bridge the gap between ancient wisdom and contemporary understanding but also to illuminate the timeless nature of Socratic thought.

Socrates' defense before the Athenian jury is more than a mere historical account; it is a profound discourse on the nature of virtue, the value of self-knowledge, and the essence of a life well-lived. By questioning the moral and intellectual complacency of his time, Socrates challenges us to examine our own beliefs, to understand the foundation upon which they rest, and to live a life in pursuit of truth and goodness.

In translating this work, I endeavored to capture the vibrancy and immediacy of Socrates' discourse. Ancient Greek, with its nuanced meanings and conceptual richness, presents a formidable challenge to the translator. My aim was to convey the depth and subtlety of the original dialogue while making it accessible and engaging for a modern audience. This meant not only choosing words that reflect the original intent but also crafting sentences that carry the rhetorical force and philosophical depth of Socrates' defense.

"The Defense of Socrates" is not just a book for philosophers or students of classical antiquity. It is a book for anyone who seeks to understand the foundation of Western thought and the enduring questions about justice, truth, and the good life. Socrates' commitment to living a life of inquiry and his ultimate sacrifice in the service of truth continue to inspire and challenge us to think deeply about our own values and the society in which we live.

As you embark on this journey through the pages of "The Defense of Socrates," I invite you to engage with Socrates' words as if he were speaking directly to you, across the millennia. Let his defense be a call to examine not only the world around you but also the innermost parts of your own mind and soul. In doing so, may you find, as I have, a source of inexhaustible wisdom and inspiration.

THE DEFENSE OF SOCRATES

{17A}[1] MEN OF ATHENS, I DO NOT KNOW HOW MY ACCUSERS have affected you. As for me, they nearly made me forget myself, so persuasively did they speak. And yet, they have scarcely uttered a word of truth. But of the many lies they told, one in particular surprised me: when they said that you must be on your guard lest you be deceived {17b} by me, as I am a skilled speaker. The fact that they are not ashamed, even though they will immediately be refuted by me in deed when I show myself to be not at all skilled in speaking—this seemed to me the height of their audacity. Unless, of course, they call one who speaks the truth a skilled speaker; if they mean this, I would agree that I am an orator, but not after their manner.

Now they, as I say, have spoken little or nothing that is true, but from me you will hear the whole truth—not, by Zeus, men of Athens, speeches finely tricked out with words and phrases, {17c} or adorned, as theirs are, but you will hear things spoken at random with the words that happen to occur to me. For I trust that what I say is just, and let none of you expect anything else. It surely would not be fitting, gentlemen, for one of my age to come before you like a youngster, molding his speeches.

And so, men of Athens, I urgently beg and beseech you: if you hear me making my defense with the same words with which I have been accustomed to speak both in the marketplace at the bankers' tables, where many of you have heard me, and elsewhere, {17d} do not be surprised or create a disturbance on this account. For the fact is, I am now making my first appearance in court at the age of seventy. I am therefore simply a stranger to the manner of speaking here.

Just as you would, of course, pardon me if I were in fact a foreigner and spoke in that dialect and manner {18a} in which I had been brought up, so now I make this request of you, a fair one, as it seems to me: disregard the manner of my speech—for perhaps it might be worse and perhaps better—and consider and pay attention merely to this: whether what I say is just or not. For that is the virtue of a judge, while an orator's virtue is to speak the truth.

{18b} Men of Athens, it is only right that I should first defend myself against the earlier false accusations and my initial accusers, before addressing the more recent ones. For many have been accusing me to you for years now, speaking untruths, whom I fear more than Anytus and his associates, formidable though they are. But the others are even more dangerous, gentlemen. They gained your belief by seizing hold of most of you in childhood, and accused me falsely, saying, "There is a certain Socrates, a wise man, a ponderer over the things in the sky and one who has investigated all things under the earth, and who makes the weaker argument the {18c} stronger." These men, Athenians, who have spread this rumor, are my most dangerous accusers. For their hearers believe that those who investigate such matters do not even believe in the gods.

Moreover, these accusers are many and have been at it a long time. They spoke to you at an age when you were most inclined to believe them, some of you being children and youths, and they won their case by default, as there was no defense. What is most unreasonable is that {18d} it is not even possible to know and name them, except when one happens to be a comic poet[2]. All those who persuaded you through envy and slander—and some also persuaded others because they themselves had been persuaded—all these are most difficult to contend with. It is not even possible to call any of them here to cross-examine them. One must simply offer a defense and refute their claims with no one responding, as if fighting with shadows.

Therefore, understand, as I say, that my accusers are of two kinds: those who have recently accused me, and the old ones I am discussing now. You should realize that I must first defend myself against the latter, for you heard them attacking me earlier, and to a much greater extent than the more {18e} recent ones. Well then. I must make my defense, men of Athens, and attempt to remove from your minds in a short time the slander that you have long held. I wish that this would be the outcome, if it is better both for you and for me, and that my defense will succeed, but I think this is difficult and I am well aware of the challenge. Nevertheless, let the matter proceed as the god may wish, but I must obey the law and present my defense.

{19a} Well then, men of Athens, I must now defend myself and attempt to clear away, in this short time, the slander that you have held against me for so long. I would wish for this to turn out well, if it is better both for you and for me, and for my defense to accomplish something. But I think this will be difficult, and I am not entirely unaware of the challenge. Nevertheless, let the outcome be as God wills; I must obey the law and present my defense.

Let us then take up from the beginning what the accusation is from which {19b} this slander against me has arisen, the very thing that Meletus trusted in when he wrote out this indictment. What exactly did my slanderers say in their slander? As if they were accusers, one must read out their sworn statement: "Socrates does wrong and is a meddlesome busybody, investigating the things beneath the earth and in the heavens, making the weaker argument the {19c} stronger, and teaching others these same things." Something like this is what they say.

Indeed, you yourselves saw these things in Aristophanes' comedy—a certain Socrates being carried around there, claiming to walk on air and spouting much other nonsense about matters of which I understand nothing, either great or small. And I do not say this to dishonor such knowledge, if someone is wise about such things—may I never have to face so many lawsuits from Meletus! But the fact is, men of Athens, I have no part in these things.

{19d} And I offer as witnesses most of you yourselves, and I ask you to inform and tell each other, those of you who have ever heard me conversing—and many of you are such people. So tell each other if any one of you has ever heard me discussing such matters to any extent at all. I contend you will find that no one has. From this you will realize that the other things said about me by the majority are of the same kind.

{19e} But none of these things are true. And if you have heard from anyone that I attempt to educate people and charge a fee for it, that is not true either. Although I do think it would be wonderful if someone were able to educate people, as Gorgias of Leontini, Prodicus of Ceos, and Hippias of Elis can. For each of these men, gentlemen, has the ability to go into any city and persuade the young men there—who can freely associate with anyone they want among their fellow citizens—{20a} to leave the company of others and join with them instead, paying money and being grateful to them besides.

Indeed, there is another wise man from Paros who I learned is in town, for I happened to run into a man who has spent more money on sophists[3] than everyone else combined—Callias, the son of Hipponicus. So I asked him, since he has two sons, "Callias," I said, "if your sons were colts or calves, we could hire an overseer for them who would make them excel in their proper virtues and qualities, {20b} and he would be a horse trainer or a farmer. But since they are human beings, who do you have in mind to oversee them? Who is an expert in this kind of excellence, in human and social virtue? I assume you must have given thought to this since you have sons. Is there someone," I asked, "or not?"

"Certainly there is," he replied.

"Who is he?" I said. "What is his name, where is he from, and what does he charge?"

"Evenus of Paros, Socrates," he replied, "and he charges five minae[4]."

{20c} And I considered Evenus blessed if he truly possesses this art and teaches it so reasonably. I myself would be puffed up with pride if I had this knowledge, but I do not have it, men of Athens.

{20d} Perhaps one of you might say, "But Socrates, what is this trouble you've gotten yourself into? Where have these slanderous accusations against you come from? Surely all this rumor and talk would not have arisen if you had simply gone about minding your own business like other people.

You must have been engaged in some unusual activity. Tell us what it is, so we won't jump to our own conclusions about you."

I think this is a fair request, so I will try to explain to you what has caused this reputation and given rise to these slanders. Listen carefully. Some of you may think I'm joking, but I assure you I will tell you the whole truth. The fact is, men of Athens, I have acquired this reputation on account of nothing more than a certain kind of wisdom. What kind of wisdom, you ask? The kind that is perhaps uniquely human. It may be that I really am wise in this limited sense. The men I just mentioned may actually possess a wisdom greater than human wisdom, or else I don't know how to describe it, because I certainly don't have it myself. Whoever claims I do is lying and speaking out of malice toward me.

{20e} Now, gentlemen, please don't interrupt me, even if you think what I'm saying sounds boastful. The words I speak are not my own; I will refer you to a trustworthy source for their truth. I will give you the god of Delphi[5] as a witness of my wisdom, if indeed it is wisdom, and of what it is. You know Chaerephon, of course. He was my friend from youth, and a friend to most of you as well. He shared in your recent exile and return. {21a} And you know what kind of man Chaerephon was, how impulsive in any course of action. He went to Delphi at one point and boldly asked the oracle—as I say, gentlemen, don't interrupt—he asked if any man was wiser than I. The Pythia[6] replied that no one was wiser. Chaerephon is dead, but his brother will testify to you about this.

{21b} Consider then why I mention these things; for I am going to explain to you how the prejudice against me has arisen. When I heard the oracle's reply, I pondered it at length, asking myself: "What in the world does the god mean? What riddle is he posing? For I am not aware of possessing any wisdom, great or small. So why then does he declare me the wisest? Surely he does not speak falsely, for that would be improper for him."

I was deeply perplexed as to his meaning for quite some time. But at last, after much reluctance, I embarked on an investigation of the matter, proceeding in this way: I went to one of those reputed to be wise, {21c} thinking that there, if anywhere, I could refute the oracle and say to it: "This man is wiser than I, but you said I was wisest."

So I carefully examined the man - I need not mention him by name, but he was one of our politicians. {21d} And this was my experience with him, my fellow Athenians - in conversing with him, this man seemed to be wise in the eyes of many people and especially in his own eyes, but he was not really so. I then tried to show him that he thought himself wise, but was not. As a result, I became hateful to him and to many of those present.

As I walked away, I reasoned to myself: "I am wiser than this man, for neither of us appears to know anything worthwhile; but he imagines he knows something when he does not, whereas I, as I do not know anything, do not imagine I do either. At any rate it seems that I am wiser than he in this one small respect: that I do not imagine I know what I do not know."

From him I went to another who was supposedly wiser, {21e} and I formed the very same impression. And there again I incurred the hostility of that man and many of his associates.

{22a} After this, I proceeded to investigate systematically, perceiving with pain and fear that I was becoming hated, but nevertheless it seemed necessary to regard the god's oracle as of the greatest importance. So I had to go, examining the meaning of the oracle, to all those who had any reputation for knowledge.

And by the dog[7], men of Athens—for I must tell you the truth—I experienced something like this: those with the highest reputation seemed to me to be nearly the most deficient, as I investigated at the god's behest, while others with a lesser reputation seemed to be wiser. I must recount to you my wanderings, as if performing labors, so that the oracle's pronouncement might be proven irrefutable to me.

After the politicians, I went to the poets - the writers of tragedies, dithyrambs, and the others - {22b} expecting that there I would catch myself being more ignorant than they. So, picking up the poems which I thought they had labored over the most, I would question them as to the poems' meanings, so that I might learn something from them at the same time.

I am ashamed to tell you the truth, gentlemen, but it must be said. Almost any of the bystanders might have spoken better than the poets themselves about the very poems they had composed. So I quickly recognized this about the poets as well: that they do not compose their works from wisdom, {22c} but from some inborn talent and by inspiration, like seers and prophets who also say many fine things without any understanding of what they say. The poets seemed to me to have experienced something similar. At the same time I saw that, because of their poetry, they considered themselves very wise men in other respects, which they were not. So I departed from there too, thinking that I had the same advantage over them as I had over the politicians.

{22d} Finally, I went to the craftsmen, for I was aware that I knew practically nothing, while I knew that I would find them knowledgeable in many fine things. And in this, I was not deceived; they knew things I did not know and were wiser than me in that respect. But, men of Athens, the skilled craftsmen seemed to me to have the same fault as the poets: because each practiced his craft well, he considered himself to be wisest in other most important matters as well. {22e} And this error of theirs obscured their wisdom, so that I asked myself, on behalf of the oracle, whether I would prefer to be as I am, neither wise in their wisdom nor ignorant in their ignorance, or to have both of the qualities they possess. I answered myself and the oracle that it is better for me to be as I am.

As a result of this investigation, men of Athens, {23a} I incurred much hatred of the most difficult and grievous kind, which has caused many slanders against me. And I gained the reputation of being wise, for in each case, those present thought that I myself was wise in the matters in which I refuted another. But the truth is, gentlemen, that the god is really wise, and by his oracle, he meant this: that human wisdom is of little or no value. And it appears that he does not actually speak of Socrates, but merely uses my name as an example, as if he were to say: {23b} "This man among you, mortals, is wisest who, like Socrates, understands that his wisdom is truly worth nothing."

Therefore, even now, I continue this investigation as the god bade me, and I go about seeking and searching for any citizen or foreigner whom I think wise. Then, if I do not think he is wise, I come to the assistance of the god and show him that he is not wise. {23c} Because of this occupation, I do not have the leisure to engage in public affairs to any extent, nor to attend to my private affairs, but I live in great poverty because of my service to the god.

{23d} In addition to this, the young men who follow me around - those with the most leisure, the sons of the wealthy

- take pleasure in hearing people being questioned. They often imitate me themselves, attempting to examine others. In doing so, I imagine they find an abundance of people who think they know something but actually know little or nothing.

As a result, those whom they examine are angry with me, not with themselves. They say, "Socrates is a most abominable person and is corrupting the youth." When someone asks them, "How? By doing and teaching what?" they have nothing to say, as they do not know. However, to avoid seeming at a loss, they resort to those stock charges commonly leveled against all philosophers: that I teach about "things in the heavens and beneath the earth," that I "do not believe in the gods," and that I "make the weaker argument the stronger." I believe they are reluctant to tell the truth - that they are exposed as pretending to have knowledge while actually knowing nothing.

{23e} Being ambitious, violent, and numerous, and speaking vehemently and persuasively about me, they have long filled your ears with fierce slanders. From among them, Meletus attacked me, along with Anytus and Lycon - Meletus angered on behalf of the poets, Anytus on behalf of the craftsmen {24a} and politicians, and Lycon on behalf of the orators. So, as I said at the beginning, I would be amazed if I could remove this prejudice from you in so short a time, given how entrenched it has become.

This, men of Athens, is the truth. I am hiding nothing from you, great or small, nor holding anything back. Yet I know well that by saying these very things, I am incurring hatred from my accusers. But this is also proof that I am speaking the truth, and that this prejudice against me exists, and these are its causes. {24b} If you investigate these matters, either now or in the future, this is what you will find.

{24c} Let this suffice as my defense against the charges of my earlier accusers. I will now attempt to defend myself against Meletus—that good and patriotic man, as he claims—and my later accusers. So once more, let us examine their sworn statement as if they were a different group of accusers. It goes something like this: Socrates is guilty of corrupting the youth and of not believing in the gods the city believes in, but in other new spiritual beings. That is the substance of the accusation. Let us examine each point of this charge one by one.

Meletus says that I am guilty of corrupting the young. But I say, men of Athens, that Meletus is guilty of treating a serious matter with levity, recklessly bringing people to trial, and pretending to be deeply concerned about things he has never cared about at all. I will try to prove to you that this is so. Come here, Meletus, and tell me: {24d} do you not consider it of the utmost importance that our young men be of the best character possible?

"I certainly do."

Come then, tell the jury who improves the youth? It is clear that you know, since you care about it. You say you have discovered the one who corrupts them—me—and you bring me here before the jury and accuse me. Come now, name the one who makes them better and inform the jury who he is. —You see, Meletus, that you are silent and unable to say. And yet, does it not seem shameful to you and sufficient proof of my point that you have never cared about this? But tell me, my good man, who makes the youth better?

{24e} But that's not what I'm asking, my good man. I'm

asking what person has this knowledge of the laws in the first place?

"These men here, Socrates. The judges."

What are you saying, Meletus? These men are able to educate the youth and make them better?

"Most certainly."

All of them, or only some?

"All of them."

{25a} By Hera, that's excellent news! We have an abundance of people who can improve the youth. But what about the audience? Do they make the youth better or not?

"They do, too."

And what about the members of the Council?

"The Council members, too."

But surely, Meletus, the members of the Assembly don't corrupt the youth, do they? Or do they also all make them better?

"They do, too."

Then it seems that all the Athenians make the youth noble and good, except for me. I alone corrupt them. Is that what you're saying?

"That is most definitely what I'm saying."

You have condemned me to a great misfortune indeed! But answer me this: {25b} Do you think it's the same with horses? That all men improve them, while one individual corrupts them? Or is the complete opposite true - that one person, or very few (the horse trainers), can improve them, while the majority of people corrupt horses if they use them and spend time with them? Isn't that the case, Meletus, both with horses and all other animals? Of course it is, whether you and Anytus say so or not. It would be a great stroke of luck for the youth if only one person corrupted them, while everyone else improved them. {25c}

But you have made it abundantly clear, Meletus, that you have never given a thought to the youth. You plainly show your own negligence, since you have not cared at all about the matters for which you bring me to trial.

{25d} Tell us further, Meletus, by Zeus: Is it better to live among good citizens or bad ones? Answer the question, my friend, for I am not asking anything difficult. Do not the wicked do some harm to those closest to them, while the good do some good?

"Certainly,"

Is there anyone, then, who would rather be harmed than benefited by his associates? Answer, my good man, for the law requires you to answer. Is there anyone who wants to be harmed?

"Of course not."

Well then, are you bringing me here on the charge of corrupting the youth and making them worse voluntarily or involuntarily?

"Voluntarily, I say."

{25e} What then, Meletus? Are you, at your age, so much wiser than I at mine, that you have recognized that the wicked always do some harm to those nearest them, while the good do good? But have I reached such a pitch of ignorance that I do not even know this: that if I make any of my associates wicked, I run the risk of getting some harm from them? And yet I bring about this great evil voluntarily, as you claim? I do not believe you, Meletus, and I do not think anyone else will believe you either. {26a} Either I do not corrupt them, or if I do, it is involuntarily, so that you are lying in either case.

But if I corrupt them involuntarily, the law does not require one to bring people to court for such unintentional wrongdoings. Rather, you should take them aside privately to teach and admonish them. For clearly, if I learn better, I will cease doing what I am doing involuntarily. But you avoided associating with me and instructing me, being unwilling to do so. Instead, you bring me here, where the law states those in need of punishment should be brought, not those in need of learning.

{26b} But indeed, men of Athens, it is now clear, as I was saying, that Meletus has never cared about these matters in the slightest. Nevertheless, tell us, Meletus, how do you claim that I corrupt the youth? Is it not obvious that, according to the indictment you brought, it is by teaching them not to acknowledge the gods the city acknowledges, but other new spiritual beings? Is this not what you say I teach, and so corrupt them?

"Absolutely, that is emphatically what I say."

Well then, Meletus, by the very gods of whom we are speaking, explain to me and these gentlemen here even more clearly. For I cannot understand whether you are saying that I teach them to acknowledge some gods—and therefore I myself do acknowledge gods and am not completely atheistic, nor do I do wrong in that way—just not the same ones as the city, but different ones, and this is the charge you bring against me, that they are different; or whether you assert that I do not acknowledge any gods at all, {26c} and that I teach this to others.

"That is what I say—that you do not acknowledge gods at all." {26d}

My remarkable Meletus, why do you say this? Do I not even acknowledge the sun or moon as gods, as other people do?

"No, by Zeus, gentlemen of the jury, he does not, since he says that the sun is a stone and the moon is earth."

Do you think you are accusing Anaxagoras, dear Meletus? Do you so despise the jury and think them so uneducated as not to know that the books of Anaxagoras of Clazomenae are full of these theories? The young men are learning these things from me, which they could sometimes buy for a drachma at most {26e} from the orchestra seats, and then laugh at Socrates if he pretended they were his own - especially since they are so absurd! But tell me, by Zeus, do I seem to you to believe that no god exists?

"Not in the slightest, by Zeus."

You are untrustworthy, Meletus, and I think you don't even trust yourself here. Men of Athens, this man seems to me to be utterly insolent and unrestrained, and to have brought this indictment simply out of insolence, lack of restraint, and youthful impulsiveness. {27a} For he seems to be composing a riddle, as if to test: "Will the wise Socrates realize I am jesting and contradicting myself, or will I deceive him and the others who hear me?" In his indictment, this man appears to me to contradict himself, as if he were to say: "Socrates is guilty of not believing in gods, but believing in gods." This is surely the jest of a jester!

Examine together with me, gentlemen, how he appears to me to be saying these things. And you, Meletus, answer us. And you, jurors - as I asked of you at the beginning - please remember not to make a disturbance if I make my arguments in my usual manner. {27b}

{27c} Tell me, Meletus, is there anyone who believes in human activities but not in humans? Let him answer, gentlemen, and not be disruptive with irrelevant objections. Is there anyone who does not believe in horses, but believes in equestrian activities? Or who does not believe flute-players exist, but believes in flute-playing? There is not, most excellent man. If you are unwilling to answer, I will tell you and the others here. But at least answer the next question: is there any person who believes in spiritual activities but not in spirits?

"There is not."

How you have benefited me by hardly answering, compelled by these gentlemen! So you assert that I believe in and teach about spiritual things, whether new or old, but at any rate that I do believe in spiritual things according to your argument. And you even swore to this in your indictment. But if I believe in spiritual things, I must quite inevitably also believe in spirits, must I not? It is so. For I assume you to be in agreement, since you do not answer. {27d} And do we not believe the spirits to be either gods or children of gods? Do you agree or not?

"Certainly."

Well then, if I believe in spirits, as you assert, and if spirits are gods of some sort, then this would be what I say you are hinting at and teasing me about - that I do not believe in gods, yet on the other hand I do believe in gods, since I believe in spirits. But if on the other hand the spirits are certain illegitimate children of gods, either by nymphs or by certain others, as indeed they are said to be, what person would believe children of gods to exist, but not gods? {27e} For it would be just as absurd as if someone were to believe that mules are the offspring of horses and donkeys, but not believe that horses and donkeys exist! But Meletus, there is no way that you brought this indictment to test us, or because you were at a loss for some true wrongdoing of which to accuse me. You must have had some other motive. But there is no way you could persuade anyone with even a little sense that the same person could believe in spiritual and divine things and yet not believe in spirits, gods, or heroes.

{28a} It is simply not possible.

{28b} But in truth, men of Athens, I do not believe it requires much of a defense to demonstrate that I am not guilty of the charges in Meletus' indictment. What I have said is sufficient. But as I stated earlier, I have incurred great hatred from many people. You know very well this is true. And this is what will convict me, if I am convicted - not Meletus or Anytus, but the slander and envy of the multitude. These have convicted many other good men too, and I think they will continue to do so. There is no danger that they will stop with me.

Perhaps someone might say: "Are you not ashamed, Socrates, to have pursued a path that has now put you at risk of death?" But I would reply to him with a just argument: "You do not speak well, sir, if you believe a man of even a little merit ought to consider the danger of life or death, rather than simply considering this when he acts - whether his actions are right or wrong, and whether they are the acts of a good or a bad man. {28c} For by your reasoning, all the demigods who died at Troy would be deemed worthless, including the son of Thetis[8], who so despised danger compared to enduring any disgrace. When his mother, a goddess, saw him eager to slay Hector, she said to him something like this, I believe: 'My child, if you avenge the death of your comrade Patroclus and kill Hector, you will die yourself. For straightaway,' she says, 'after Hector, death is ready for you.' Hearing this, he made light of death and danger, fearing much more to {28d} live as a coward and not avenge his friends. He says, 'May I die at once after imposing justice on the wrongdoer, so that I might not remain here, a laughingstock by the curved ships, a burden upon the earth.' Do you think he considered death and danger?"

{28e} For the truth is this, men of Athens: wherever a

man takes his stand, believing it to be the best course, or is stationed there by his commander, there he is bound to remain and face the danger, without considering death or any other peril in comparison with dishonor. {29a} It would be a dreadful thing indeed if I, having faced death at the posts you yourselves appointed me to, at Potidaea, Amphipolis, and Delium, were now to desert my station out of fear of death or any other danger—the very station the god has placed me at. For that would justly summon me to court on the charge of disbelieving in the gods, disobeying the oracle, and fearing death above all else. In truth, men, to fear death is simply to think oneself wise when one is not, to think one knows what one does not know. No one knows whether death may not be the greatest of all blessings for a man, yet men fear it as if they knew with certainty that it is the greatest of evils. {29b} And is this not the most blame-worthy ignorance, to think one knows what one does not know? In this, perhaps I differ from the majority of men, and if I were to claim to be wiser than anyone in anything, it would be in this: that not adequately knowing the things of the underworld, I do not presume to know them. But I do know that it is wicked and shameful to do wrong, to disobey one's superior, whether god or man. I shall never fear or avoid things which, for all I know, may be good, in prefer-ence to evils which I know to be evils.

{29c} So if you were to acquit me now, disregarding Anytus who declared that either I should never have been brought to trial at all, or that now that I have been, I must be put to death—if you were to say to me: "Socrates, we shall disregard Anytus and acquit you, but only on condition that you abandon your search for truth and your philosophy. If you are caught doing this again, you shall be put to death"—if you were to offer me release on those terms, I would reply:

{29d} Men of Athens, I appreciate and love you, but I shall obey the god rather than you, and as long as I draw breath and have my faculties, I shall never stop practicing philosophy, exhorting anyone I meet and saying in my usual way: "You, a citizen of the great and mighty city of Athens, are you not ashamed to care only for the acquisition of wealth, reputation, and honor, while neglecting the perfection of your reason and your soul?" {29e} And if any of you argues this point and claims to care about these higher things, I shall not immediately let him go or leave him. I shall question, examine, and test him. And if I find that he does not possess virtue but merely says he does, I shall rebuke him for scorning what is of greatest value and caring more for what is of lesser worth. {30a} I shall treat in this way anyone I happen to meet, young and old, citizen and stranger, and more so the citizens because you are more kindred to me.

Know that this is the command of the god, and I believe that no greater good has ever come to pass in the city than my service to the god. For I go about doing nothing else than urging you, young and old, not to care for your bodies or your wealth more than for the perfection of your souls, {30b} telling you that virtue does not come from money, but from virtue comes money and all other good things, both to the individual and to the city. If by this teaching I corrupt the youth, then this advice must be harmful. But if anyone asserts that I teach anything else, he is talking nonsense. Therefore, men of Athens, I say to you, do as Anytus bids or not as Anytus bids, and either acquit me or not; but whichever you do, understand that I shall never alter my ways, {30c} not even if I have to die many times.

{30d} Men of Athens, do not be disruptive, but abide by my request to not make a disturbance at my words and instead hear me out. For I believe you will benefit from listening. I am about to tell you some other things at which you may cry out, but please, do not do this. Know well that if you kill me, being such a man as I say I am, you will not harm me more than yourselves. For neither Meletus nor Anytus could harm me - they couldn't, as I don't think it's permitted by the divine for a better man to be harmed by a worse. Perhaps they might kill, exile, or disfranchise me - things which they and maybe others consider great evils. But I don't think so; rather, I believe doing what they're doing now - attempting to unjustly execute a man - is a much greater evil.

So now, men of Athens, I am far from making a defense speech for my own sake, as one might expect, but rather for yours - to prevent you from wrongdoing by misjudging me and the gift the god gave you in me. {30e} For if you kill me, you will not easily find another like me, who - even if it's rather ridiculous to say - has simply been attached to this city by the god, as if to a large and well-bred horse that is rather sluggish due to its size and needs to be awakened by some gadfly. It's as if the god has stationed me as something of the sort to the city, to awaken, persuade and reproach each one of you, {31a} settling in everywhere and not stopping the whole day.

Such a man will not come to you easily again, gentlemen. But if you heed me, you will spare me. However, perhaps you may be irritated, like drowsy people awakened, and strike me - persuaded by Anytus, you may thoughtlessly kill me. If you do, then you would spend the rest of your lives asleep, unless the god, caring for you, should send you someone else. That I happen to be the sort of person given to the city by the god, you might realize from this: {31b} It does not seem human that I have neglected all my own affairs and put up with the neglect of my household all these years, always tending to your needs, approaching each of you individually like a father or older brother, persuading you to care for virtue. If I profited from this by charging a fee for my advice, there would be an explanation. But now you see for yourselves that my accusers, though shamelessly charging me with everything else, could not bring themselves to produce a witness showing {31c} that I ever exacted or requested a fee. I think I provide sufficient witness that I speak the truth: my poverty.

{31d} Now, it may seem strange that I go around privately giving this advice and meddling in others' affairs, yet do not venture to come before your assembly and advise the city publicly. The reason for this, as you have heard me say on many occasions, is that something divine and supernatural comes to me. This began when I was a child—a sort of voice that comes to me, and whenever it does, it always dissuades me from what I am about to do, but never encourages me. This is what opposes my engaging in politics, and I think its opposition is absolutely right.

For you may be sure, men of Athens, that if I had long ago attempted to take part in politics, I would have perished long ago, without doing any good either to you or to myself. {31e} Please don't be offended by my telling the truth, but the fact is that no man will preserve his life for long who genuinely opposes either you or any other multitude and prevents many unjust and illegal things from happening in the city. Rather, {32a} anyone who really fights for justice, if he is to preserve his life for even a short time, must act as a private citizen, not a public one.

I will give you powerful proofs of this, not mere words, but what you value—deeds. Listen to what happened to me, so that you may know that I would never yield to any man contrary to what is right, for fear of death, even if I should die at once for not yielding. The things I will tell you are commonplace and smack of the lawcourts, but they are true.

{32b} The only office I ever held in the city, men of Athens, was that of councilor. The tribe Antiochis, to which I belong, held the presidency when you wanted to try as a body the ten generals who had failed to pick up the survivors of the naval battle[9]. This was illegal, as you all recognized later. At that time I alone of the presidents opposed doing anything contrary to the laws, and I voted against it. The orators were ready to prosecute me and take me into custody, and you were urging them on with shouts, but I thought I should run any risk on the side of law and justice rather than join you, {32c} for fear of prison or death, when you were engaged in an unjust course.

This happened while the city was still a democracy. When the oligarchy was established, the Thirty[10] summoned me to the Hall, along with four others, and ordered us to bring Leon the Salaminian from Salamis to be executed. They often gave such orders to many people, in order to implicate as many as possible in their crimes. On that occasion, however, I showed again, not in words but in action, {32d} that I do not care about death in the least—if it's not too crude to say so—but that I do care with all my might about not doing anything unjust or impious. That government, powerful as it was, did not frighten me into any wrongdoing. When we left the Hall, the other four went to Salamis and brought back Leon, but I simply went home. I might have been put to death for this, had the government not fallen shortly afterwards. There are many who will testify to these events.

{33a} Men of Athens, do you really think that I could have survived all these years if I were engaged in public affairs, and acting as a good man must, came to the aid of justice and considered this the highest priority? Far from it, Athenians. No other man could have survived either.

But throughout my life, in any public activity I may have engaged in, I am the same man as I am in private life. I have never conceded anything to anyone contrary to what is just, neither to any others, nor to any of those who my accusers say are my students. I have never been anyone's teacher. If anyone, young or old, desires to listen to me speaking and pursuing my own mission, I have never begrudged this to anyone. {33b} I do not converse only when I receive money and not when I do not receive it, but I offer myself as a questioner to rich and poor alike. And if any of them wishes to answer and then listen to what I have to say, I am ready for that as well.

Now if any of them turns out to be a good man or not, I would not be justly held responsible, since I never promised or gave any instruction to any of them. If someone claims to have learned or heard anything privately from me which everyone else did not, be assured he is not telling the truth.

{33c} But why then do some enjoy spending considerable time with me? You have heard the reason, Athenians. I told you the whole truth. They enjoy hearing those being questioned who think they are wise but are not. And this is indeed rather amusing. But I say that this duty has been assigned to me by the god[11] through oracles, dreams, and in every other way that a divine mandate has ever ordered a man to do anything whatsoever.

This, Athenians, is both true and easily verified. {33d} For if I am corrupting some of the young and have corrupted others, then surely some of them who have grown older and realized that I gave them bad advice when they were young would now come forward to accuse me. If they were unwilling to do so themselves, then some of their family members—fathers, brothers, or other relatives—would recall it now and seek punishment on my behalf.

Many of them are present here today, whom I see: first Crito, my contemporary and fellow member of the deme[12] of Alopece, father of Critobulus here; next, Lysanias of Sphettus, father of Aeschines here; also, Antiphon of Cephisia, father of Epigenes; {33e} then there are others whose brothers spent time in this way—Nicostratus son of Theozotides and brother of Theodotus (Theodotus is dead, so he could not influence him), and Paralus here, son of Demodocus, whose brother was Theages; and Adeimantus, {34a} son of Ariston, whose brother is Plato here; and Aeantodorus, whose brother Apollodorus is present.

I could mention many others, some of whom Meletus should have called as witnesses in his own speech. If he forgot then, let him do so now—I yield the floor to him—and let him say if he has any such evidence. But you will find, gentlemen, that the exact opposite is true. They are all ready to come to the aid of me, the alleged corrupter, the one who supposedly harms their family members, as Meletus and Anytus claim.

Now those who were corrupted might have reason to help me, but what motive do the uncorrupted have, {34b} the older men who are their relatives, to aid me other than the right and just motive, that they know Meletus is lying and I am speaking the truth?

{34c} So be it, gentlemen. This, and perhaps a bit more like it, is nearly all I would have to say in my defense. But perhaps one of you may feel resentful upon recalling how he himself, even when involved in a far less dire trial than this, begged and pleaded with the judges, shedding many tears and parading his children before the court to arouse the utmost pity, along with many of his family and friends -

whereas I will do none of these things, even though I may seem to be facing the ultimate danger.

With this in mind, someone might adopt a more stubborn attitude towards me and, angered by that very conduct, cast his vote in anger. {34d} Now if any of you feels this way - I do not expect it, but just in case - I think it would be fair for me to reply to him, "My good sir, I too have some family, for as Homer says, I am not 'born from oak or rock' but from human parents. And so, men of Athens, I have family - three sons, one already a youth and two still children. But nonetheless, I will not bring any of them here to beg you to acquit me."

Why then will I do none of these things? Not from arrogance, Athenians, {34e} nor from disrespect towards you. As for whether I face death with confidence or not, that is another matter. But for the sake of my reputation and yours, and that of the whole city, I do not think it proper for me to do any of these things at my age and with my name - whether deserved or not - for it is generally believed that Socrates is in some way superior to most men.

{35a} It would be shameful if those of you who are considered superior, whether in wisdom, courage or any other virtue, should behave in that way. I have often seen men facing trial who, though they have some reputation, act in astonishing ways as if they thought it a terrible thing to die - as if they would be immortal if you did not execute them! In my view, these men bring shame upon the city, so that even a foreigner might assume that those Athenians who excel in virtue, and whom the people choose for their own offices and other honors, are no better than women. {35b} This, men of Athens, we ought not to do, we who have any reputation at all. And if we do, you ought not to allow it. Rather, you should make it very clear that you will be much more likely to condemn a man who puts on these pitiful dramatics and makes the city a laughingstock, than one who keeps his composure.

{35c} But apart from the question of reputation, gentlemen, it does not seem right to me to beg the jury or to seek acquittal through pleading; rather, one should inform and persuade them. The juror does not sit in order to grant justice as a favor, but to determine where justice lies. He has sworn not to show favor at his own discretion, but to judge according to the laws. Therefore, we should not accustom you to disregard your oath, nor should you make a habit of doing so. {35d} It would be impious for either of us to do this.

So do not expect me, men of Athens, to act towards you in a way that I consider dishonorable, unjust, or impious—especially, by Zeus, when I am being prosecuted by Meletus here on a charge of impiety! For clearly, if I were to persuade you and overpower your oath by begging, I would be teaching you to believe that there are no gods, and in making my defense I would be accusing myself of not believing in them. But that is far from the truth. I do believe in the gods, men of Athens, more than any of my accusers. And I entrust to you and to the god[13] to judge me in the way that will be best for me and for you.

{35E} Now, men of Athens, I am not angry at the verdict you have reached, for many reasons. {36a} What has happened was not unexpected to me; indeed, I am much more surprised at how close the vote was on each side. I did not think the decision would be by such a narrow margin, but by a large one. But now, it seems, if only thirty votes had gone the other way, I would have been acquitted.

In fact, I think that I would have escaped Meletus and his charges even now. And not only would I have escaped, but it is clear to all that if Anytus and Lycon had not joined him in accusing me, {36b} Meletus would have been fined a thousand drachmas for not receiving a fifth of the votes[14].

{36c} The man has proposed death as my penalty. Very well. What, then, shall I propose as a counter-penalty, men of Athens? Clearly, it must be what I deserve. So then, what do I deserve to suffer or to pay, because I did not keep quiet in my life? Rather than concerning myself with what most people care about—making money, managing a household, gaining military rank, speaking in the Assembly, and pursuing the other offices, political clubs, and factions that exist in the city—I went where I believed I could do the greatest good for each of you individually. {36d} I tried to persuade each of you not to care for any of your own possessions until you have cared for yourself, striving to be as good and wise as possible. I urged you not to care for the city's possessions until you have cared for the city itself, and to care for other things in the same way. What, then, does a man such as myself deserve? Some good thing, men of Athens, if I must truly propose a penalty according to my deserts—and a good thing of such a kind as would be fitting for me.

What is fitting for a poor man who is your benefactor, one who needs leisure to exhort you? There is nothing more fitting, men of Athens, than for such a man to be given his meals in the Prytaneum[15]. {36e} This is much more appropriate for me than for any of you who has won a victory at Olympia with a horse, a chariot, or a team of horses. For he makes you seem to be happy, whereas I make you truly happy. He is not in need of sustenance, whereas I am in need of it. {37a} So if I must assess the penalty fairly according to my deserts, I assess it at this: free meals in the Prytaneum.

{37b} Perhaps, men of Athens, what I am saying now strikes you as similar to my arguments against appeals for sympathy and pleading for mercy - merely a display of arrogance. But that is not the case at all. Rather, the truth is this: I am convinced that I never wrong anyone willingly, but I have failed to convince you of this, for we have conversed with each other only a short time. I believe if you had a law, as some others do, not to decide a capital case in a single day but over many, you would be persuaded. As things stand, it is not easy to dispel serious slanders in such a short time.

Being convinced, then, that I wrong no one, I am hardly going to wrong myself by asserting that I deserve some evil and proposing a penalty of that sort for myself. What would I fear? That I might suffer the penalty Meletus proposes, which I say I do not know whether it is good or bad? Instead of that, should I choose something I know very well to be an evil and propose that as a penalty? Imprisonment? {37c} Why should I live in prison, enslaved to the Eleven[16] who are always in charge? A fine, and imprisonment until I pay it? But that is the same as what I just said, for I do not have any money to pay a fine with.

Shall I then propose exile as my penalty? Perhaps you would accept that. But I would have to be exceedingly fond of life, men of Athens, to be so irrational as to suppose that while you, my fellow citizens, could not endure my discussions and arguments - finding them so burdensome and odious that you are now seeking to be rid of them - others will cheerfully tolerate them. {37d} Far from it, men of Athens. It would be a fine life for me at my age to be driven out from one city to another, constantly changing my place of residence. For I know well that wherever I go, the young men will listen to my teachings, just as they do here. If I drive them away, they will persuade their elders to expel me. {37e} If I do not drive them away, their fathers and relatives will expel me on their account.

{38a} Perhaps someone might say: "But Socrates, if you leave us, could you not live a quiet life, without talking?" This is the hardest thing of all to make some of you believe. For if I say that such conduct would be disobedience to the god and that therefore I cannot keep quiet, you will think I am not being serious. If on the other hand I tell you that the greatest good a man can have is to discuss virtue every day and those other things about which you hear me conversing and testing myself and others, for the unexamined life is not worth living, you will believe me even less. Yet that is the truth, gentlemen, though it is not easy to persuade you.

Besides, I am not accustomed to thinking of myself as deserving any punishment. {38b} If I had money, I would have proposed a fine that I could afford, for that would have done me no harm. But as it is - I have no money, unless you are willing to impose a fine within my modest means. I might perhaps pay you one minae of silver. So that is my proposal.

But, men of Athens, Plato here and Crito and Critobulus and Apollodorus tell me to propose a fine of thirty minas, and they guarantee payment. So that is my proposal, and they will be sufficient guarantee of the money.

{38c} IT WILL NOT BE LONG, Athenians, before you acquire a reputation and incur censure from those who wish to disparage our city, for having put to death Socrates, a wise man - for they will call me wise even though I am not, these detractors who want to reproach you. If you had waited just a little while, this would have happened of its own accord anyway. For you see my age, that I am already advanced in years and close to death. I say this not to all of you, {38d} but only to those who voted for my execution. And to them I also say this: perhaps you think, gentlemen, that I have been convicted through a lack of words - words that might have persuaded you, if I had thought it right to do and say anything to avoid the penalty. Far from it. I have been convicted because I lacked not words but boldness and shamelessness and the willingness to say to you what you would most gladly have heard from me, lamentations and tears and my saying and doing many things that I say are unworthy of me but that you are accustomed to hear from others. {38e} But I did not think then that the danger I faced should make me do anything dishonorable, nor do I now regret the nature of my defense. I would much rather die after this kind of defense than live after making the other kind.

Neither in a lawsuit nor in battle should I or anyone else contrive to escape death at any cost. {39a} Indeed, in battle it is often obvious that a man might avoid death by throwing down his weapons and begging for mercy from his pursuers. And there are many other ways to escape death in every kind of danger if one is willing to do or say anything to avoid it. But it is not death, gentlemen, that is difficult to escape, but wickedness, {39b} for wickedness runs faster than death. And now I, being slow and old, have been caught by the slower pursuer, while my accusers, being clever and quick, have been caught by the faster one, wickedness. And now I depart, sentenced by you to death, while they are sentenced by truth to depravity and injustice. I abide by my penalty, and they by theirs. Perhaps these things had to happen this way, and I think they are as they should be.

{39c} Men who have condemned me, I would now like to foretell what will happen after this. For I am at the point where men most frequently prophesy—when they are about to die. I say to you, my executioners, that immediately after my death a punishment far more painful than the sentence you passed on me shall befall you, I swear by Zeus. You have done this deed supposing you will be free from having to give an account of your lives, but I say the result will be quite the opposite. There will be more people to test you, whom I have been holding back until now, {39d}though you did not notice it. And they will be harsher because they are younger, and you will be even more indignant.

If you think that by killing men you will prevent anyone from reproaching you for not living rightly, you are mistaken. This way of escaping is neither possible nor honorable. The easiest and noblest way is not to suppress others but to make yourselves as good as possible. With this prophecy to you who voted against me, I take my leave.

{39e} But to those who voted for my acquittal, I would gladly speak about this thing that has happened, while the authorities are busy and before I must go to the place of my execution. Wait with me for this short time, my friends. Nothing prevents us from conversing with each other while it is still permitted.

{40a} I want to explain to you, as friends, the meaning of what has befallen me. O my judges—for you I may truly call judges—a wonderful thing has happened to me. The divine sign that I am accustomed to, my spiritual guide, was previously very frequent, always opposing me even in small matters if I was about to do something wrong. But now that

I am in the situation you see, which one might think is the worst of evils, the sign of the god has not opposed me, {40b} either when I left home this morning, or when I came up here to the court, or at any point during my speech when I was about to say something. Yet in other talks it often held me back in the middle of my speaking, but now it has never opposed me in any part of this affair, in anything I was doing or saying. What then do I suppose is the reason? I will tell you. What has happened to me is likely a good thing, and we are surely mistaken in supposing death to be an evil. {40c} I have strong evidence of this, for my customary sign would certainly have opposed me if I were not about to do something good.

Let us also consider in this way how there is much hope that death is a good thing. For death is one of two things: either the dead are nothing and have no perception of anything, or as we are told, it is a change and a relocating for the soul from here to another place.

And if it is complete lack of perception, like a dreamless sleep, then death would be a great advantage. For I think that if someone, having picked out a night during which he slept {40d} without even dreaming, and then compared it to all the other nights and days of his life, and had to say, upon reflection, how many days and nights he had lived better and more pleasantly than that night - I think that not just an ordinary person, but even the great King[17] himself would find these to be few in number compared to the other days and nights. So if death is like this, I say it is an advantage, {40e} for all eternity would then seem to be no more than a single night.

If, on the other hand, death is a change from here to another place, and what we are told is true, that all the dead are there, what greater blessing could there be than this, gentlemen of the jury? {41a} For if someone arriving in Hades, having escaped these who claim to be jurors, will find those who are true judges who are said to sit in judgment there - Minos and Rhadamanthys and Aeacus and Triptolemus and the other demigods who were just in their own lives - would that be a poor kind of change?

Or again, what would one of you give to keep company with Orpheus and Musaeus, Hesiod and Homer? I am willing to die many times if these things are true, since I personally would find the conversation there immensely rewarding, {41b} when I could meet Palamedes and Ajax, son of Telamon, and any other of the men of old who lost their lives through an unjust conviction. And there would be no small pleasure, I think, in comparing my experience with theirs.

And the greatest pleasure would be to spend my time there, as here, examining and searching people's minds, to find out who among them is wise and who thinks he is, but is not. What would one not give, gentlemen of the jury, to be able to question the leader of the great Trojan expedition[18], {41c} or Odysseus, or Sisyphus, or countless other men and women one could mention? It would be an extraordinary happiness to talk with them, to keep company with them and examine them.

In any case, they would certainly not put one to death for doing so. For besides being happier than we are in other respects, they are immortal for the rest of time, if indeed what we are told is true.

{41d} But you too must be of good hope in the face of death, gentlemen of the jury, and keep this one truth in mind: no evil can befall a good man, either in life or after death, and his affairs are not neglected by the gods. What has happened to me now has not occurred by chance;

rather, it is clear to me that to die now and be freed from my troubles was what was best. This is why my divine sign - my inner voice that warns me against harmful actions - did not oppose me at any point, and why I am not at all angry with those who condemned me or with my accusers. And yet, it was not with this thought that they condemned and accused me, but because they believed they were harming me. {41e} For this, they deserve blame.

However, I make this request of them: when my sons grow up, punish them, men, by troubling them in the very same ways I troubled you, if they seem to care for money or anything else above virtue. And if they think they amount to something when they are really worth nothing, reproach them just as I reproached you, for not caring about what they ought, and for thinking they are worthy when they are worthless. {42a} If you do this, both I and my sons will have received just treatment at your hands.

But now the hour to part has come. I go to die, and you to live. Which of us goes to the better lot is known to no one, except to the god.

NOTES

The Defense of Socrates

1. Stephanus pagination is a reference system for Plato's works based on the 1578 three-volume edition by Henricus Stephanus. It uses page and section numbers for precise citations (e.g. 17a), dividing Plato's texts into sections for easy reference. The system allows for unique citations with the work's name, page number, and section letter. Despite its specificity, the system has peculiarities, such as variable page and paragraph lengths and missing sections.
2. I.e. Aristophanes, who satirized Socrates in his play "The Clouds".
3. Teachers of rhetoric and philosophy.
4. A mina was equivalent to 100 drachmas which was a considerable sum.
5. Apollo, whose oracle was located at Delphi
6. The priestess of Apollo at Delphi.
7. An oath.
8. Achilles
9. Of Arginusae in 406 BC.
10. Tyrants who ruled Athens for a short period in 404 BC
11. Apollo.
12. Local district.
13. Apollo.
14. Tthe minimum required to avoid a fine for bringing a frivolous lawsuit.
15. The city hall where honored guests dined at public expense.
16. The prison guards.
17. Of Persia.
18. Agamemnon.

www.ingramcontent.com/pod-product-compliance
Lightning Source LLC
Chambersburg PA
CBHW021404160726
47994CB00007B/3071

To K & C Your laughter and love infuse every page of "*The Adventures of the Kindness Club: Discovering the Superpowers Within*." This book is a testament to the joy you bring into my life. May its message of kindness inspire your own adventures, and may you always carry the superpowers of compassion and empathy in your hearts.

Rasha Zeitoun

THE ADVENTURES OF THE KINDNESS CLUB: DISCOVERING THE SUPERPOWERS WITHIN

AUSTIN MACAULEY PUBLISHERS™

LONDON • CAMBRIDGE • NEW YORK • SHARJAH

Copyright © Rasha Zeitoun 2024

The right of Rasha Zeitoun to be identified as author of this work has been asserted by the author in accordance with Federal Law No. (7) of UAE, Year 2002, Concerning Copyrights and Neighboring Rights.

All rights reserved. No part of this publication may be reproduced, stored in a retrieval system, or transmitted in any form or by any means, electronic, mechanical, photocopying, recording, or otherwise, without the prior permission of the publishers.

Any person who commits any unauthorized act in relation to this publication may be liable to legal prosecution and civil claims for damages.

ISBN – 9789948747215 – (Paperback)
ISBN – 9789948747222 – (E-Book)

Application Number: MC-10-01-3420239
Age Classification: 10-12

The age group that matches the content of the books has been classified according to the age classification system issued by the UAE Media Council.

First Published 2024
AUSTIN MACAULEY PUBLISHERS FZE
Sharjah Publishing City
P.O Box [519201]
Sharjah, UAE
www.austinmacauley.ae
+971 655 95 202

This journey through the pages of "*The Adventures of the Kindness Club: Discovering the Superpowers Within*" has been a collaborative odyssey filled with warmth, growth, and shared aspirations. To the members of the Kindness Club, both fictional and the real-life inspirations around me, your spirit and compassion have shaped this narrative into a tale of enduring friendship and empathy. I extend my deepest gratitude to Dale Carnegie, whose timeless principles have been a guiding light, infusing this story with profound lessons on human relations. To my family, your unwavering support has been my anchor throughout this creative venture. A special appreciation goes to the dedicated educators and parents who strive to instill kindness in the hearts of the next generation. Your commitment to nurturing empathy is the heartbeat of this book. This literary voyage wouldn't be complete without acknowledging the readers—the true adventurers. May the kindness within these pages resonate with you, inspiring a ripple effect of compassion and positive change. Thank you for joining me on this transformative journey. With heartfelt gratitude.

Prologue
The Call to Kindness

In the vibrant town of Greenville, nestled amidst rolling hills and blooming meadows, there was a special group of young friends who believed in the power of kindness. They called themselves the Kindness Club and little did they know that they were about to embark on extraordinary adventures that would change their lives and the lives of those around them.

Each member of the Kindness Club possessed unique qualities that made them special.s Sammy, the leader, had a heart overflowing with compassion. Emma, with her infectious laughter, could brighten anyone's day. Max had a way of making everyone feel included and valued. Sophie's imaginative storytelling brought enchantment to their world. And there was Lee, Hana, Celine, Layla, Omar, and many others, each with their own remarkable strengths.

One sunny day, as the Kindness Club gathered under their favorite oak tree, a gentle breeze carried a whispered message through the air. It was as if the wind itself had become a messenger, spreading the call to kindness throughout Greenville.

"Children of Greenville," the wind whispered, "a great task awaits you. The world is in need of your special gifts. It is time for you to discover the superpowers within and embark on the most incredible adventure of all—to create a safe and kind environment, where no one is ever subjected to the hurtful claws of bullying."

As the Kindness Club listened, their eyes widened with anticipation and determination. They realized that they had the power to make a difference, to stand up against bullying and create a world where kindness reigned supreme.

But they also understood that this journey wouldn't be easy. They would face challenges, doubts, and obstacles along the way. The wind's whisper carried a solemn reminder— they would need to embrace the teachings of a wise mentor who had long ago illuminated the path to human connection and understanding.

With hearts united and a shared purpose, the Kindness Club made a solemn vow under the oak tree. They would embark on a quest to embrace and practice the nine principles of human relations, inspired by the teachings of Dale Carnegie. These principles would serve as their guide, their armor, and their superpowers:

- The Power of Not Criticizing
- The Power of Appreciation
- The Power of Not Complaining
- The Power of Showing Genuine Interest
- The Power of Smiles
- The Power of Remembering Names
- The Power of Listening
- The Power of Talking in Terms of Other People's Interests
- The Power of Making Others Feel Important

With the wind as their ally and the teachings of Dale Carnegie as their compass, the Kindness Club stood tall, ready to face any challenge that lay ahead. They would become the heroes of Greenville, spreading kindness, empathy, and love wherever they went.

Little did they know that their adventures would take them on a rollercoaster ride of emotions, introducing them to unique individuals and teaching them life lessons that would shape their character and leave an indelible mark on their hearts.

And so, with hearts brimming with hope and determination, the Kindness Club prepared to embark on the extraordinary journey that awaited them. They were destined to discover the superpowers within, and in doing so, they would change not only their lives but also the world around them.

The Adventures of Kindness Club had just begun, and the stage was set for a tale of compassion, friendship, and the triumph of kindness over cruelty. The journey promised to be filled with magic, challenges, and life-altering lessons, as the Kindness Club set out to create a world where bullying had no place and kindness reigned supreme.

And so, dear friend, join us.

Chapter 1
The No-Criticism Crew

In a small town named Greenville lived a kind-hearted boy named Sammy. Sammy was always eager to help others and spread joy wherever he went. One day, he came up with a brilliant idea to form a special club called the Kindness Club. His goal was to gather like-minded friends who believed in the power of kindness and being friendly people.

Sammy reached out to his friends and shared his idea. They were all excited to join the Kindness Club and make the world a better place. Together, they became known as the No-Criticism Crew because they had a rule to never criticize, condemn, or complain.

As the No-Criticism Crew, Sammy and his friends discovered that words could have a tremendous impact on other people. They learned that by choosing kind and uplifting words, they could bring happiness to others and create a positive environment.

One sunny day, the No-Criticism Crew faced their first challenge. Their dear friend, Alex, was feeling down and couldn't see the bright side of things. Sammy knew that it was the perfect opportunity for the No-Criticism Crew to make a difference.

Sammy gathered his friends and they brainstormed ways to help Alex. They knew that criticizing or complaining about Alex's negative attitude wouldn't solve the problem. Instead, they decided to use the power of kindness and understanding.

They organized a surprise picnic in the park, with colorful balloons, delicious snacks, and a heartwarming message for Alex. When Alex arrived at the park, they greeted him with warm smiles and open arms. Sammy, as the leader of the No-Criticism Crew, stepped forward and spoke gently to his friend.

"Alex," Sammy said, "we understand that things might seem tough right now, but we want you to know that we're here for you. We believe in the power of positivity and kindness. Let's try to find the bright side together."

As they shared stories, played games, and laughed together, the No-Criticism Crew showed Alex that life had many beautiful moments. They encouraged him to focus on the things that brought him joy and helped him see the silver lining in every situation.

Days turned into weeks, and Alex gradually started to embrace the positive outlook that the No-Criticism Crew had shown him. With their unwavering support, he realized that he could overcome challenges with a smile on his face and kindness in his heart.

Word about the No-Criticism Crew spread throughout Greenville, and more children joined the Kindness Club. Together, they created a community that celebrated kindness and uplifted others.

And so, the No-Criticism Crew continued their mission, spreading kindness and understanding to everyone they met.

Sammy and his friends taught the world that a little kindness could change lives and make the world a better place.

From that day forward, the No-Criticism Crew became a shining example of how to see the bright side of things, even during tough times. And they continued to inspire children far and wide to join their club and be a part of the wonderful world of kindness.

Chapter 2
The Kindness Club's
Magical Compliments

The No-Criticism Crew, now known as the Kindness Club, continued their mission to spread joy and kindness throughout Greenville. One sunny day, as they walked along the colorful streets, they noticed a girl sitting alone on a park bench, her shoulders slumped and a frown on her face.

The Kindness Club approached the girl, and Sammy, the leader, kindly asked, "Hello there, is everything okay?"

The girl looked up with teary eyes and explained that she was feeling sad and unimportant. She believed that nobody noticed or appreciated her for who she was. The Kindness Club knew that this was an opportunity to make a difference.

Emma, one of the club members, approached the girl and spoke with a warm smile. "You know, I've always admired your beautiful voice. Your singing brings so much joy to those who hear it."

Max, another club member, added, "And your artwork is simply amazing! The way you use colors and shapes to express your emotions is truly inspiring."

Sophie, the storyteller of the group, chimed in, "Your imagination is incredible! The stories you create are like magic, and they transport us to wonderful new worlds."

As each member of the Kindness Club shared heartfelt compliments, the girl's face lit up. She had never realized that her talents and unique qualities were so appreciated by others. The Kindness Club's words of appreciation were like a ray of sunshine that lifted her spirits.

Encouraged by the girl's growing smile, the Kindness Club continued to shower her with compliments, highlighting her kindness, empathy, and ability to make others feel loved and supported. With each word, the girl's self-confidence grew stronger.

Together, they spent the afternoon playing games, laughing, and sharing stories. The girl felt a sense of belonging as the Kindness Club embraced her for who she truly was.

Chapter 3
The Want Warriors

The Kindness Club had become a beacon of positivity and compassion in their small town. Sammy and his friends were always looking for new ways to uplift others and spread kindness. One day, as they gathered for their weekly meeting, Sammy shared an idea he had come across: the power of arousing an eager want in others.

"Guys, I read about a concept called 'arousing an eager want'," Sammy said with excitement. "It's about helping someone discover their true passions and desires and then supporting them to pursue those dreams."

The Kindness Club listened attentively, eager to learn more about this new approach to kindness. They knew it was another opportunity to make a positive impact on someone's life.

A few days later, while walking through the town square, the Kindness Club spotted a hesitant girl named Nadine. She was watching a group of talented dancers practicing their routines for an upcoming dance competition. Nadine's eyes sparkled with admiration, but there was a hint of sadness and self-doubt in her gaze.

The Kindness Club approached Nadine, and Sammy gently asked, "Nadine, we couldn't help but notice your interest in the dance competition. Is there something you'd like to share with us?"

Nadine hesitated for a moment, her voice barely above a whisper. "I… I've always wanted to dance, but I'm too afraid to join the competition. I don't think I'm good enough."

The Kindness Club understood Nadine's fear and knew it was the perfect opportunity to put their newfound knowledge into action. They gathered around her, offering their support and encouragement.

Emma, with her kind smile, said, "Nadine, your passion for dance shines through your eyes. We believe in you, and we know that you have the potential to be an amazing dancer."

Max added, "Your dedication and hard work will take you far. Don't let self-doubt hold you back from pursuing your dreams."

Sophie, the storyteller, stepped forward and said, "Nadine, imagine the joy and fulfillment you'll experience when you step onto that stage, expressing yourself through dance. It's a magical feeling that only you can bring to life."

Nadine looked at her friends, her eyes welling up with tears of gratitude. She had never felt such unwavering support and belief in herself. The Kindness Club's words had awakened a fire within her, and she began to see the possibilities that lay ahead.

With the Kindness Club by her side, Nadine started attending dance classes, practicing her moves, and building her confidence. They cheered her on during every step of her journey, reminding her of her unique talents and the joy she brought to others through her dancing.

As the day of the dance competition approached, Nadine's nervousness resurfaced. But the Kindness Club was there to remind her of the progress she had made and the incredible dancer she had become.

On the day of the competition, Nadine stood backstage, her heart pounding with anticipation. She took a deep breath, remembering the unwavering support of the Kindness Club. With newfound confidence, she stepped onto the stage and let the music guide her movements.

Nadine's performance was breathtaking. Her passion and dedication were evident in every graceful step. The audience was captivated by her talent and the sheer joy she radiated on stage.

When the applause filled the auditorium, Nadine knew she had not only conquered her fear but had also inspired others with her courage. The Kindness Club rushed to her side, enveloping her in a warm embrace.

From that day forward, Nadine continued to pursue her passion for dance, always supported by the Kindness Club.

Chapter 4
The Curiosity Crusaders

The Kindness Club had embarked on a new mission: to become genuinely interested in other people and their stories. They understood that by listening with their hearts and minds, they could create meaningful connections and make a positive impact.

One day, while exploring the local library, the Kindness Club stumbled upon a shy girl named Hana. Hana was sitting in a cozy corner, surrounded by stacks of books. She had a notebook in her lap, filled with her own handwritten tales.

Intrigued by Hana's presence, Sammy approached her with a warm smile.

"Hi, Hana! We couldn't help but notice your love for storytelling. Would you mind sharing one of your tales with us?"

Hana blushed and hesitated for a moment before opening up her notebook. With a soft voice, she began to narrate a magical adventure filled with brave heroes, mythical creatures, and lessons of kindness. As she spoke, her eyes sparkled with excitement, and her words carried the power to transport the listeners to a world of imagination.

The members of the Kindness Club sat around Hana, captivated by her storytelling. They listened attentively, hanging on to every word and encouraging her with their warm expressions. They genuinely wanted to know more about her stories and the inspiration behind them.

After Hana finished her tale, Emma praised, "Hana, your storytelling is enchanting! I felt like I was right there alongside the characters, experiencing their triumphs and challenges."

Max added, "Your attention to detail and vivid descriptions bring your stories to life. You have a true gift for capturing the imagination of your audience."

Sophie, the storyteller of the Kindness Club, expressed, "Hana, your tales inspire kindness and courage. They have the power to touch the hearts of many, and I believe your stories deserve to be shared with a wider audience."

Hana's face lit up with a mixture of surprise and joy. She had always been shy about sharing her stories, but the genuine interest and encouragement from the Kindness Club gave her the confidence to consider sharing her tales beyond the pages of her notebook.

In the following weeks, the Kindness Club continued to meet with Hana, eagerly listening to her new stories and providing feedback that celebrated her unique storytelling style. They encouraged her to participate in local storytelling events and even organized a special storytelling evening where Hana could showcase her talents to a supportive audience.

As Hana shared her stories with others, she realized the impact her words had on the listeners. Children and adults alike were captivated by her storytelling, and her tales spread a sense of wonder, kindness, and imagination throughout the community.

With the continued support of the Kindness Club, Hana blossomed into a confident storyteller. She no longer hid behind shyness but embraced her gift, knowing that her stories had the power to inspire and uplift others.

The Kindness Club had not only created a bond with Hana but had also ignited her passion for storytelling and helped her find her voice. Together, they celebrated the beauty of storytelling and the magic that can be found in genuine curiosity and appreciation for others.

And so, the Curiosity Crusaders of the Kindness Club continued their mission, spreading kindness and embracing the unique talents and stories of those they encountered. They inspired others to be genuinely interested in people, to listen with open hearts, and to celebrate the diverse gifts that make each individual special.

Chapter 5
The Smiling Squad

The Kindness Club, now known as the Smiling Squad, continued their journey of spreading joy and kindness throughout Greenville. One day, as they walked along the streets, they noticed a girl named Layla sitting alone on a bench, her head bowed and a frown on her face. It was evident that she was feeling sad.

Sammy, the leader of the Smiling Squad, approached Layla with a warm smile. "Hi, Layla," he said gently, "is everything okay?"

Layla looked up, surprised by the kindness in Sammy's eyes. She sighed and explained that she was feeling down and overwhelmed by life's challenges. The Smiling Squad knew that this was an opportunity to make a difference.

Emma, a member of the squad, stepped forward and said, "Layla, we believe in the power of smiles. Sometimes, a simple smile can brighten someone's day and remind them that they are not alone."

Max, another member, added, "Even in difficult times, a smile can bring a ray of hope and happiness. Let us show you."

With that, the members of the Smiling Squad began to smile brightly at Layla. At first, Layla was taken aback, but she couldn't help but be affected by their warm and genuine smiles. Slowly, a small smile tugged at the corners of her lips.

Feeling encouraged, Sophie, the storyteller of the group, shared a lighthearted joke that made Layla chuckle. Layla's smile grew wider, and a spark of joy returned to her eyes.

Inspired by Layla's response, the Smiling Squad decided to spread smiles throughout the town. They greeted people with warm smiles, offered compliments, and performed small acts of kindness. They visited the local park, where children were playing, and their smiles ignited laughter and happiness among the youngsters.

The Smiling Squad's enthusiasm was infectious, and soon the entire town of Greenville was caught up in the spirit of smiling. People who had been feeling down or stressed began to smile more often, and the town became a happier and friendlier place.

As for Layla, her smile became a permanent fixture on her face. She found solace and strength in the Smiling Squad's unwavering support and the positive environment they had created. Layla realized that even in tough times, a simple smile could make a difference, not only in her own life but also in the lives of those around her.

The Smiling Squad's message of spreading joy and kindness through smiles resonated with the community. More people joined their cause, and the Smiling Squad grew into a movement that brought smiles to people's faces far and wide.

From that day forward, the Smiling Squad continued to be a beacon of positivity, spreading smiles and uplifting spirits wherever they went. Their simple yet powerful message reminded everyone of the importance of kindness, compassion, and the transformative power of a smile.

And so, the Smiling Squad, with Layla by their side, continued their mission to create a happier and more united community. They showed the world that a genuine smile has the power to brighten someone's day, heal wounds, and create a ripple effect of kindness and joy.

Chapter 6
The Name Knights

The Kindness Club, now known as the Name Knights, embarked on a new mission to understand the importance of remembering names. They believed that by acknowledging and remembering someone's name, they could make others feel important and valued. Their latest challenge came when they met a forgetful boy named Omar.

Omar always seemed to struggle with remembering names, often causing him embarrassment and making others feel overlooked. The Name Knights recognized that this was an opportunity to make a difference in Omar's life.

Approaching Omar with kindness and empathy, Sammy, the leader of the Name Knights, said, "Hey, Omar! We've noticed that remembering names can sometimes be tricky. But we have a few creative techniques that might help you recall names more easily."

Intrigued, Omar looked at Sammy with a mixture of hope and curiosity. He expressed his desire to remember names and make others feel important, just like the Name Knights did.

Max, a member of the Name Knights, shared a technique he had learned. "Omar, imagine each person's name as a picture. When you meet someone, try to picture their name written on a colorful, vibrant painting. This visual image can help you associate the person's face with their name."

Emma, another member, added, "Another trick is to repeat the person's name when you first meet them and use it in conversation. This repetition will reinforce the name in your memory and show the person that you care about them."

With the guidance of the Name Knights, Omar practiced these techniques diligently. Whenever he met someone new, he would visualize their name as a vibrant picture and repeat it several times in conversation. Gradually, Omar's ability to remember names improved, and he began to feel more confident and valued.

To further support Omar, the Name Knights decided to organize a special event. They invited Omar's friends, family, and classmates to a gathering where everyone wore name tags. This allowed Omar to practice his newfound skills in a friendly and supportive environment.

During the event, the Name Knights made sure to use everyone's names repeatedly, making each person feel seen and appreciated. Omar embraced the opportunity to engage with others, calling them by their names and sparking conversations that revealed the unique stories behind each person.

As the event unfolded, Omar's efforts and the Name Knights' support began to bear fruit. People noticed and appreciated Omar's genuine interest in getting to know them. The Name Knights showed Omar that remembering names went beyond a mere skill—it was an act of kindness and a way to make others feel valued and respected.

From that day forward, Omar continued to improve his memory and practiced the techniques taught by the Name

Knights. With their guidance, he became known for his ability to remember names and make everyone he encountered feel important.

The impact of the Name Knights' mission extended beyond Omar. The community, inspired by their efforts, started paying closer attention to names, recognizing the value they held in building connections and fostering a sense of belonging. The Name Knights' message of name-recognition kindness spread far and wide, transforming the town of Greenville into a place where everyone felt seen, heard, and appreciated.

And so, the Name Knights, with Omar as their shining example, continued their mission to make every person they met feel important and valued through the power of remembering names. Their dedication to this simple yet profound act of kindness left a lasting impact on the hearts of Greenville's residents, forging stronger bonds and fostering a sense of community.

As they journeyed forward, the Name Knights knew that remembering names was not just about words—it was a symbol of respect, empathy, and the power to make a difference in someone's life. They pledged to continue their quest, ensuring that no name went forgotten and that everyone they encountered felt like a cherished member of their kingdom of kindness.

Chapter 7
The Listening League

The Kindness Club, now known as the Listening League, discovered the power of becoming expert listeners. They understood that lending an ear and truly hearing someone could make them feel understood and less lonely. Their latest encounter led them to a chatty girl named Hana, who often felt unheard and overlooked.

One day, as the members of the Listening League strolled through Greenville, they noticed Hana sitting alone on a park bench, speaking animatedly to herself. They approached her with warm smiles and open hearts, ready to listen.

"Hi, Hana!" Sophie, a member of the Listening League, greeted her. "We've noticed you have a lot to say. Would you like to share your thoughts with us?"

Hana looked up, surprised and intrigued by their genuine interest. She had always felt as though her words fell on deaf ears, but the Listening League's invitation gave her a glimmer of hope.

With a mixture of excitement and hesitation, Hana began to pour out her thoughts and feelings. She shared her dreams, her fears, and the stories that played in her imagination. The members of the Listening League listened attentively, nodding and affirming her experiences.

As Hana spoke, she felt a sense of validation and understanding. The Listening League's genuine interest and unwavering attention made her feel seen and valued. They didn't interrupt or rush her; instead, they encouraged her to express herself freely.

Max, a member of the Listening League, asked thoughtful questions and reflected back on Hana's words, showing that he truly understood what she was conveying. Emma and Sammy, the leaders, offered words of encouragement and support, fostering an atmosphere of trust and openness.

Through their active listening, the Listening League helped Hana realize that her voice mattered. They showed her that her thoughts and feelings were valid and deserving of attention. Hana, in turn, grew more confident in expressing herself and embraced her uniqueness.

In the following days, the Listening League continued to spend time with Hana, actively listening to her stories, ideas, and emotions. They created a safe space where she felt comfortable and understood. Their genuine interest in her thoughts and feelings blossomed into a deep friendship.

Inspired by Hana's resilience and creativity, the Listening League encouraged her to share her stories and thoughts with others in Greenville. They organized storytelling sessions in the park, where Hana captivated audiences with her imaginative tales.

As the town embraced Hana's storytelling, she found a sense of belonging and connection. The Listening League's support and active listening had given her the confidence to share her gifts with the world.

Word of the Listening League's empathetic listening skills spread throughout Greenville. The community recognized the power of truly hearing one another, and conversations became more meaningful and compassionate. The Listening League's mission to create a culture of attentive listening transformed the town into a place where everyone felt heard and understood.

And so, the Listening League, with Hana's stories weaving their way into the hearts of Greenville's residents, continued their mission to be expert listeners. They knew that by offering their ears and hearts to those who felt unheard, they could make a profound impact on individuals and the community.

As they journeyed forward, the Listening League celebrated the power of listening to foster empathy, understanding, and connection. They pledged to keep their ears open and their hearts ready, ensuring that no voice went unnoticed, and no person felt alone in their thoughts and emotions. The Listening League, with Hana's friendship and storytelling as their guiding lights, would forever be the champions of attentive listening in the town of Greenville.

Chapter 8
The Interests Investigators

The Kindness Club, now known as the Interests Investigators, had come to understand the importance of speaking in terms of other people's interests. They knew that by showing genuine curiosity and embracing diverse hobbies, they could celebrate individuality and forge lasting friendships. Their latest adventure led them to a girl named Celine, who had a wide range of hobbies and interests.

One sunny day, as the Interests Investigators explored Greenville, they came across Celine sitting under a tree, engrossed in a book about astronomy. Intrigued by her passion, they approached her with smiles on their faces.

"Hi, Celine!" Max, a member of the Interests Investigators, greeted her. "We noticed you're into astronomy. That's fascinating! Can you tell us more about it?"

Celine looked up, pleasantly surprised by their interest in her hobby. She shared her love for stargazing, learning about the universe, and her dreams of becoming an astronaut. The Interests Investigators listened attentively, asking questions and showing a genuine curiosity about her passions.

As the conversation unfolded, the Interests Investigators discovered that despite having different hobbies themselves, they could still find common ground with Celine. They shared stories of their own adventures, from hiking and camping to exploring nature and the great outdoors. It turned out that Celine had a fondness for outdoor activities as well.

Excitedly, the Interests Investigators invited Celine to join them on their next outdoor adventure. They planned a hiking trip to a nearby mountain and eagerly anticipated the opportunity to explore nature together. In doing so, they were talking in terms of Celine's interests and embracing her love for outdoor adventures.

During the hike, the Interests Investigators encouraged Celine to share more about her passion for astronomy. They listened intently as she talked about constellations, galaxies, and the wonders of the universe. They found themselves captivated by her knowledge and enthusiasm.

As they reached the mountaintop, a breathtaking view unfolded before them. Celine pointed out different stars and constellations, sharing her knowledge with the group. The Interests Investigators marveled at the beauty of the night sky, feeling a deep connection with both nature and each other.

Through their shared adventure and genuine interest in Celine's hobbies, the Interests Investigators celebrated the diversity of their interests. They learned that embracing different passions and finding common ground allowed them to forge lasting friendships based on respect, curiosity, and understanding.

From that day forward, the Interests Investigators continued to explore new hobbies and interests, encouraging one another to pursue their passions. They recognized that talking in terms of other people's interests created bridges of connection and fostered a sense of belonging within their group.

Greenville became a vibrant community where individuals were celebrated for their unique hobbies and talents. The Interests Investigators, with their open-mindedness and willingness to learn from one another, inspired others to embrace diverse interests and appreciate the richness of individuality.

As they embarked on new adventures and discovered new passions, the Interests Investigators remained committed to celebrating the diverse tapestry of interests that made their friendships stronger and their experiences more vibrant. They understood that by valuing and speaking in terms of other people's interests, they could create a world where everyone felt seen, heard, and valued for who they truly were.

Chapter 9
The Importance Impresarios

The Kindness Club, now known as the Importance Impresarios, had embarked on a new journey of making others feel important. They understood that genuine acknowledgment and appreciation could make a significant impact on someone's self-worth and happiness. Their path led them to a boy named Lee, who often felt unnoticed and unappreciated.

One sunny day, as the Importance Impresarios strolled through Greenville, they noticed Lee sitting alone on a bench, his head bowed low. They approached him with warm smiles, their hearts brimming with a desire to uplift his spirits.

"Hello, Lee," Sammy, the leader of the Importance Impresarios, greeted him. "We've noticed all the amazing things you do, and we want you to know that you are truly valued."

Lee looked up, surprised by their words. He often felt like his efforts went unnoticed, so hearing such a heartfelt statement touched him deeply. The Importance Impresarios gathered around him, each sharing specific instances where they had seen his contributions and the positive impact he had on others.

Emma, a member of the Importance Impresarios, spoke up first. "Lee, your kindness knows no bounds. I remember when you helped me carry my heavy backpack when I was struggling. It made such a difference in my day."

Max added, "And let's not forget how you always take the time to listen and offer support to anyone who needs it. Your empathy is a gift that brings comfort to those around you."

Sophie, the storyteller of the group, chimed in, "Your creativity shines through in all the artwork you create. It brings joy to everyone who sees it. You have a unique talent, Lee."

As each member of the Importance Impresarios shared their genuine appreciation for Lee's qualities and actions, his face lit up. He had never realized how much he truly mattered to others. The Importance Impresarios' words of recognition and praise were like a warm embrace, filling him with a sense of worth and belonging.

Motivated by Lee's growing smile, the Importance Impresarios continued to highlight his contributions, both big and small. They encouraged him to recognize his own strengths and to believe in his abilities. They reminded him that he was an essential part of their community and that his presence made a positive difference.

In the following weeks, Lee's confidence and self-esteem blossomed. He embraced new opportunities and shared his talents with others, knowing that his efforts were valued and appreciated. The Importance Impresarios stood by his side, supporting him every step of the way.

Word about the Importance Impresarios and their mission spread throughout Greenville. More and more people began to recognize and acknowledge the importance of others, fostering a community where everyone's contributions were celebrated.

As the Importance Impresarios continued their journey, they made it their mission to ensure that no one in Greenville felt unnoticed or unappreciated. Through their genuine acknowledgment and heartfelt appreciation, they helped individuals like Lee realize their worth and understand the significant impact they had on others.

Greenville became a place where people felt seen, heard, and valued for their unique contributions. The Importance Impresarios' legacy lived on as they inspired others to recognize the importance of every individual, creating a world where kindness, appreciation, and recognition were the foundations of a thriving and compassionate community.

Join US
The Kindness Club
Saves the Day!

As the Kindness Club gathered together, reflecting on their incredible journey, their hearts were filled with gratitude and joy. They celebrated the friendships they had formed, the lives they had touched, and the positive change they had brought to Greenville.

Through their commitment to the nine principles they had discovered—from being the No-Criticism Crew to the Importance Impresarios—they had become true superheroes of kindness. They had learned the power of words, the importance of empathy, the value of genuine appreciation, and the beauty of embracing diversity.

The Kindness Club realized that their mission was not just about spreading kindness but also about inspiring others to join them on this incredible journey. They understood that kindness had the power to transform lives, heal wounds, and bring joy to even the darkest corners of the world.

With renewed determination, they turned to the young readers, eager to share their story and invite them to join the Kindness Club. They knew that by embracing these principles, the young readers could become superheroes of kindness in their own lives and make a positive impact in their communities.

They encouraged the young readers to be like Sammy, Emma, Max, Sophie, and all the members of the Kindness Club. They urged them to be the change they wished to see in the world, to spread kindness, uplift others, and make a difference wherever they went.

And so, the Kindness Club's story became an inspiration for generations to come. The young readers eagerly embraced the invitation, eager to embark on their own journey of kindness and join the Kindness Club. Together, they would create a world where compassion, understanding, and love flourished.

As the pages of their story closed, the legacy of the Kindness Club lived on. The town of Greenville thrived as a beacon of kindness and compassion, and its inhabitants, young and old, knew the power of a kind word, a helping hand, and a heart full of love.

And so, dear readers, the power to save the day and create a better world lies within each and every one of you. Will you join the Kindness Club and become a superhero of kindness? The choice is yours.

www.ingramcontent.com/pod-product-compliance
Lightning Source LLC
Chambersburg PA
CBHW021405160726
47994CB00007B/3083